JB
C 3798
D 8

MAY   2008

Uh Huh!

The Story of

Ray Charles

John Duggleby

MORGAN
REYNOLDS
PUBLISHING
Greensboro, North Carolina

1

In the summer of 1930, a pregnant teenager named Aretha Robinson slipped out of the northern Florida hamlet of Greenville. She crossed the state line to Albany, Georgia, where she stayed with relatives until her baby was born. Retha, as everyone called her, had been left alone when her mother died the year before. Her father had long since deserted the family. The pretty, petite girl had been taken in by Mary Jane Robinson and her husband, Bailey. She adopted the Robinson name and, not long after, became pregnant. It was rumored, and later confirmed, that Bailey was the baby's father.

Retha gave birth to a boy she named Ray Charles Robinson (called R. C.) on September 23, 1930. She returned to Greenville a few months later. The young

Opposite: Ray Charles *(AP Photo)*

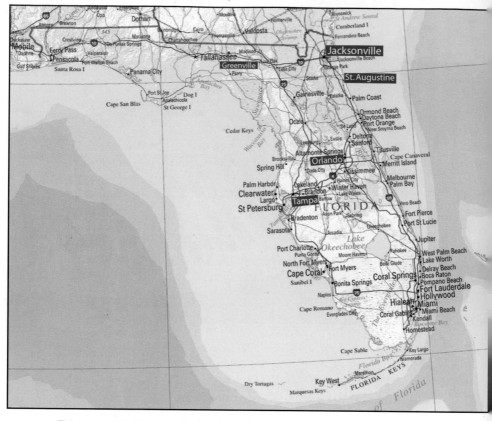

This map of Florida marks the significant places where Ray spent time while living in the state. The town of his birth, Albany, Georgia, is located about one hundred miles northwest of Greenville.

mother and her baby settled into an enclave on the edge of town called Jellyroll, the shabbiest corner of a larger area called Blackbottom, the "colored" side of town.

"Even compared to other blacks, we were on the bottom of the ladder looking up at everyone else," Ray would later recall. "Nothing below us except the ground." His frail mother took in washing and ironing work from the white people of Greenville, but she could do little else. What help she received often came from a surprising source: Mary Jane Robinson. Since Retha was barely sixteen, Mary Jane didn't hold her responsible for getting pregnant with Bailey's child. Instead, she divorced Bailey, and R. C.'s father soon drifted away.

What R. C. lost in an absentee father he gained through two caring women. Retha was a loving but strict mother. She made a long list of rules. The most important was: no matter what, never beg or steal. Mary Jane was more like an indulgent grandmother and often watched R. C. when Retha was working or sick. Mary Jane was a sturdy woman with a steady job at a local sawmill, and she spoiled young R. C. with sweets and other gifts his mother couldn't afford.

Others also took a liking to Retha and her bright-eyed boy. Someone might butcher a hog for them, and on those occasions nothing went to waste. Ray later recalled that they ate everything inside and out, from ears to feet, except the "oink." Decades later he still rhapsodized about boyhood feasts of neck bones, chitlins, collard greens, rice with onion gravy, ham chunks simmering in cabbage, and slabs of watermelon.

Wiley and Georgia Pitman ran the Red Wing Café and boardinghouse in Jellyroll, and provided Retha and her son free lodging when other options ran out. Though R. C. had to crowd into the same bed as his mother, other amenities at the Red Wing more than compensated for the hardships. Mr. Pit, as everyone called him, owned what became the two most cherished items of young R. C.'s life.

One was an old upright piano Mr. Pit used to pound out popular boogie-woogie, a rhythmic fusion of jazz and blues music just catching on in the 1930s. Mr. Pit was a local legend whose knack for hammering out rhythms with one hand and melodies with the other kept the Red Wing jumping day and night.

One day as Mr. Pit practiced he noticed three-year-old R. C. hovering nearby and hoisted the youngster onto the piano bench. The boy whacked the keyboard as hard as he could. Instead of getting angry, the old master explained, "You don't hit the keys with your fist. I'm going to show you how to play a little melody with one finger."

From that moment on, the keys of Mr. Pit's piano became the most important reason R. C. got up each day. As he hung out at the Red Wing, the mentor encouraged his young charge, saying, "Come over here, boy, and see what you can do with this pie-ano." Within a couple of years, Mr. Pit could proudly show off R. C. playing recognizable tunes for his patrons.

To R. C., the other treasure in Mr. Pit's trove was the Red Wing's juke-box. Mr. Pit loaded it with his favorite records. Some were by jazz artists such as Louis Armstrong and Duke

An early Duke Ellington record cover.

Ellington, who entertained both black and white audiences. Others were "race" records, made by African-American artists for a mostly black audience. These included not only boogie-woogie piano arrangements but stripped-down country blues numbers by black musicians with names such as Blind Boy Phillips and Washboard Slim.

When someone plugged the jukebox with change, R. C. sat on a bench with his ear practically plastered to the speaker. He had to listen to what the paying customers chose, but he didn't care; it was all red-hot to R. C. Once in a while Mary Jane gave him some pennies for candy, which he might use instead to select his own favorite songs.

When Mr. Pit or someone else played the radio, R. C. encountered a different brand of music. The airwaves then were filled with what white people wanted to hear, and in the rural South that often meant "hillbilly" music played on acoustic stringed instruments by people who sang with sometimes-mournful voices. On Saturday nights many black people tuned in to the Grand Ole Opry beamed across the South from Nashville, Tennessee.

For Retha and R. C., Sunday morning, without fail, meant service at the New Shiloh Baptist Church. The fiery preacher whipped the congregation into tears of joy and wails of ecstasy. He called to the congregation and they sang back, beating tambourines and clapping their hands. Climaxing with a chicken dinner on the grounds, Sunday morning church became as merry for R. C. as Saturday night at Mr. Pit's.

Before the Civil War, slaves found ways to endure the arduous task of working in the fields by singing call-and-response songs, often with religious themes, which came to be known as spirituals. *(Library of Congress)*

The most sacred and the most secular music of R. C.'s childhood sprang from the same source. When West African slaves first arrived in America, they brought a singing style with melodies and rhythms unlike the European musical tradition carried on by whites in the New World. Africans preferred a call-and-response technique in which an individual singer issued a "call" that was answered in unison by several others. This technique was channeled into work songs as slaves toiled in plantation fields, the rhythm sometimes set by a white overseer to increase their labor. African Americans who converted to Christianity also incorporated rhythm into spirituals, religious songs often concerning events in the Bible.

When slavery ended after the Civil War, these two musical roads stretched further. Black musicians learned to accompany their hard-luck work ballads on instruments discarded by wartime military bands, barroom pianos, or stringed instruments such as guitars or banjos they sometimes made themselves. Around 1900, this music became known as the blues and soon gave birth to the uniquely American musical forms of ragtime and, later, jazz. Blues songs were first recorded as race records specifically marketed to black listeners, not many years before R. C. first heard them on Mr. Pit's jukebox.

During the same post-Civil War era, African-American Christians began establishing their own churches. Though they drew from the same scriptures, the black religious music that became known as gospel was different from traditional white church hymns. Gospel songs often crackled with shouting and clapping—in short, sharing many similar elements with the blues.

The legendary gospel singer Mahalia Jackson. *(Library of Congress)*

Gospel music debuted on record about a decade later than the blues, but during R. C.'s boyhood, race records began to carry not just blues shouters but gospel singers such as Mahalia Jackson and the Swan Silvertones. R. C. loved both blues and gospel music, and would always consider them musical sons of the same mother.

Although Retha never married, she had another boy named George a year after R. C. was born. George and R. C. were not only half brothers but best friends. When he wasn't doing something musical, R. C. usually played with George.

The brothers became inseparable, disappearing into the piney woods for hours and surfacing only to guzzle

Kool-Aid or nurse a wound. They learned to cover a cut with clay dirt or a cobweb to stop the bleeding. For boils, they heated a brick, held it close to their skin, and poured water on it. The resulting steam caused the boil to burst. What couldn't be healed with home remedies was treated with castor oil. Retha wouldn't hear of spending money on a doctor.

George took to numbers with the same affinity and skill that R. C. took to music. By the time he was three, the younger brother had taught himself to add, multiply, and divide. Soon neighbors stopped by just to watch George solve math problems. They wondered if George might grow up to be someone like George Washington Carver, a black scientist who became famous for developing hundreds of new uses for peanuts and other crops at his lab in neighboring Alabama.

Then, everything changed. One hot summer day, when R. C. and George were five and four, they filled their mother's huge metal laundry tub with water and hopped in, clothes and all, to take a swim. Soon George was kicking and splashing, seemingly having a good time. Eventually, it dawned on R. C. that George's carrying-on was not for fun but for help. George was drowning.

For a moment, R. C. was frozen with fear. When he finally acted, he lacked the strength to drag his brother, weighed down by his wet clothes, over the steep side of the tub. He ran to the house, screaming, "Mama! Mama!" Retha pulled George from the tub and tried to revive him, breathing into his mouth and slapping his back.

Finally, she stopped and erupted with a flood of tears. R. C. didn't need to be told: George was dead.

R. C.'s happy-go-lucky demeanor faded to numbness as his brother, whose future had seemed so bright, was laid to rest. He had not only lost his constant companion but he had also been an eyewitness to George's tragic death. How could life get any worse?

Into the Darkness

2

Shortly after George's death, distant images began to blur before R. C.'s eyes. Soon, the boy awoke each day with his eyelids stuck together with mucus so thick his mother had to swab them with warm water before prying them open. They visited the only doctor in town who would treat black people, who in turn sent him to a specialist in a town fourteen miles away. The second physician broke the grim news: "I'm afraid the boy's going blind."

Retha was brokenhearted, but she knew that the worst thing for R. C. would be to surrender to despair. She insisted that he wash and dress himself, plus keep up his chores such as washing clothes, even handling an axe to chop wood. Local busybodies accused Retha of showing a callous attitude toward R. C.'s misfortune.

"He's blind," she said, "but he ain't stupid. He's lost his sight, but he ain't lost his mind." She knew that unless R. C. learned to take care of himself, he would be at everyone's mercy the rest of his life.

Retha's tough love paid off. Instead of retreating into a shell of helplessness from his troubles, Ray continued to run and play with his buddies Johnnycake, Lou Dell, Beatrice, Mary Lee, and Wilbur. He also made tracks just as frequently to the Red Wing and Mr. Pit's piano. R. C. had always enjoyed the cool texture of the ebony and ivory keys; now he truly had to learn to feel the music.

As her son was coping with his sight loss, Retha realized that R. C. had needs beyond what she could provide. For one, his sighted friends were learning to read. He would require special help to learn Braille, the system blind people use to read and write. And Retha needed the intervention of white people to connect with providers of such assistance. African Americans had little political or social clout in much of America during the 1930s.

The local doctor who first examined R. C. knew of a state school for the blind and deaf. After a wealthy Greenville couple heard R. C. play their living-room piano, they were taken by the talented blind boy and brandished their clout in a recommendation letter to the institution. R. C. was accepted as a charity student who could attend for free, which was the only way Retha could have managed. She jumped at the opportunity, and at age seven, R. C. faced leaving the only home he had ever known. He didn't take the news well.

Going blind was one thing, but leaving Retha and his surrogate mother, Mary Jane, was quite another. They were his whole world. Mary Jane didn't make it any easier. She dreaded the end of R. C.'s visits to her house and argued that he'd be better off at home with people who cared most for him and would make him more comfortable.

Retha regretted losing her son more than anyone, but she pondered the bigger picture. She, Mary Jane, and friends such as Mr. Pit wouldn't be around forever. R. C. would need to achieve independence. If he didn't learn to read and write, his prospects were grim.

So in the fall of 1937, R. C. boarded the "colored"

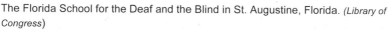

The Florida School for the Deaf and the Blind in St. Augustine, Florida. *(Library of Congress)*

section of a train bound for St. Augustine, 140 miles away. Though he didn't expect much, at first the Florida School for the Deaf and the Blind was even worse than he'd feared. Veteran students seemed bent on making the new kid's life miserable.

When R. C. bragged about how fast he could run, the upperclassmen set up a race. They developed a system in which a boy held one end of a wire while another boy held the other end about one hundred feet away. The blind contestants felt the wire as they ran to stay on course. When R. C.'s turn came, the older students quickly tied the finish end of the wire to an iron pole. R. C.'s dash ended with a crash, and the perpetrators taunted him with chants of "little sissy boy" as he cried.

R. C. also tasted his first painful dose of racism. As he left a group of white students one day, one of the boys called him a nigger. Ray later explained, "I honestly had never heard the word before, but I hated it the first time. I picked up the kid like a paper sack and dropped him." His outburst cost R. C. two weeks of dining-hall dishwashing duty, a chore typically performed only by the girls.

R. C. quickly learned that daily life at the school was literally a matter of black and white. While play was integrated, students of different races were housed in separate quarters and taught by instructors of their own color. Black students, who made up less than a quarter of the school's population, were strictly forbidden to cross the curtain of wild bamboo that separated them

The dorms where African-American students lived and studied at the Florida School for the Deaf and the Blind. *(Florida School for the Deaf and the Blind, St. Augustine)*

from white facilities. They even needed special permission to travel to the school medical center housed on white turf. "Imagine the nonsense of segregating *blind* kids," Ray would one day marvel. "I mean, they can't even see!"

R. C. soon settled into the new routine. Like Retha, school administrators set a no-nonsense regimen designed to teach blind and deaf children discipline and self-reliance. The daily schedule varied little:

> 5:30 AM: Woke up to an alarm bell. R. C. washed up with other boys in a group bathroom. He usually had a few minutes to talk with his friends before breakfast.
>
> 6:40 AM: Breakfast in the black kids' dining hall. The menu was usually oatmeal, cream of wheat, or grits with butter. The boys had milk every morning and a glass of orange juice on Mondays. Spare time after breakfast was spent finishing homework, if necessary, but R. C. much preferred tuning in to jazz on a local radio station.

7:55 AM: The first school bell rang and the children filed into the chapel. Boys sat on one side of the aisle, girls on the other. The group sang a song such as "America the Beautiful," then received a lecture from the principal of the Colored Department.

9 AM: Classes began in earnest, with the morning devoted to academic subjects. For new blind students like Ray, that meant first taking a crash course to learn Braille. After that they used Braille books to study subjects such as English and math, just like sighted kids.

1 PM: Back to the dining hall for a quick dinner. It was usually a variation of vegetables, macaroni, and potatoes and gravy, with some stew meat or a sausage thrown in.

1:30 PM: The boys went to a workshop to learn vocational skills and, incidentally, to raise money for the school. R. C.'s nimble piano-playing fingers were also great for sewing and weaving items such as leather wallets, brooms, and cane-seated chairs sold by the school.

4 PM: Students received an hour-long outside recess to do as they pleased. R. C. and his friends enjoyed a crude form of baseball using a broomstick bat and a ball made from a tightly rolled magazine.

5 PM: Supper at the dining hall, which usually consisted of bread with syrup or spaghetti. After eating, students did their homework before getting ready for bed.

9 PM: Lights out, no exceptions.

R. C. adjusted well to his new life at school. He learned Braille after two weeks and was devouring books within a couple of months. Everything was fine until Christmas when all the students returned home to visit their families—all except him. The "free ride" at the state institution included train trips only at the beginning and end of the school year. Retha couldn't afford R. C.'s train ticket home for the holidays, and the first-year student endured a heartsick two weeks alone at school.

As it turned out, the return of his friends to begin the second semester heralded an even greater pain. R. C.'s right eye began to hurt and it was soon throbbing from morning to night. He finally crossed into white territory the hard way when the school doctor hospitalized him with some bad news. There was no choice; his eye had to be removed.

Though his eyes were virtually useless, the thought of one actually being plucked out terrified R. C. He eventually returned to classes, but he was more than ready to reunite with Retha, Mary Jane, and his friends when the school year ended in June. He was welcomed back as the same old R. C., and within a few days it seemed like he'd never left.

R. C.'s return to the blind school that fall was a definite improvement over his rookie year. To his delight, he received piano lessons. The conditions weren't perfect; R. C.'s teachers favored European classical compositions over Mr. Pit's jumping boogie-woogie. R. C.

considered Bach "nervous," but he appreciated the passion of pieces such as Beethoven's *Moonlight So-nata.* "I could just feel the pain that this man was going through," he later explained. "You know that he was very, very lonesome when he wrote that."

The truth was that any music was worth tolerating because the teacher opened an entirely new door for R. C.: she taught him how to read music in Braille. Playing Braille scores wasn't easy because R. C. always needed one hand to read the bumps on the sheet music. He first had to play the piano's left-hand part while reading across the page with his right, then learn each measure by heart until he could play the entire song from memory using both hands. R. C. learned most pieces two measures at a time, an agonizingly slow process for classical selections containing as many as two hundred bars.

BRAILLE'S MIRACULOUS DOTS

Louis Braille lived a world and over a century apart from Ray Charles, but the two had much in common. Like Ray, Braille was blinded at a young age. Three years after his birth in France in 1809, the boy accidentally injured his eyes with a sharp tool in his father's harness-making shop. Braille's eyes became infected, leaving him totally blind.

Young Braille also shared Ray's love of music. He was an extremely bright boy who learned to play by listening to the piano and organ. The dedicated student eventually earned a scholarship to the Royal Institution for Blind Youth in Paris. Here, at the

Louis Braille.

world's first school for blind people, Braille learned to read from books with letters raised up on the page so students could feel them— a workable method, but not an easy one. The boy acquired reading and writing skills through this method but he was convinced that there had to be a better way.

At the same time, Charles Barbier de la Serre, a French soldier, was refining a system of tactile communication to help pass messages along when light was unavailable—or when its presence would make soldiers more vulnerable to their enemies. He brought his system to the Institution for Blind Youth. Louis Braille immediately understood the potential these raised dots and dashes held and, using his inside knowledge of how blind people can best feel information, the twelve-year-old began working on a system using different arrangements of six dots to represent each letter of the alphabet.

In three years the teenager had perfected the method that now bears his name. He soon added symbols based on his keyboard experience, and at age twenty published his *Method of Writing Words, Music and Plain Song by Means of Dots, for Use by the Blind and Arranged by Them.*

The Braille system was ingenious but also ahead of its time. Braille spent his adult life as a respected teacher and musician—he became the organist at a prominent Paris church—but he died at age forty-three without wide acceptance of his dot code. Soon after his death, educators began to advocate Braille until it became the worldwide standard for teaching blind people to read and write.

Today, Louis Braille's enlightening system has been adapted to virtually every language on the globe and for computer usage. His brilliance has opened doors for countless millions, including another blind but musical teenager who, like Braille, would eventually be called a genius.

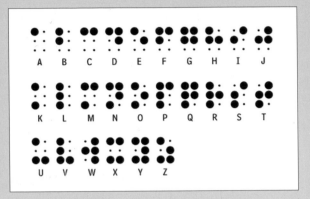

The Braille alphabet is made up of patterns of raised dots and dashes.

R. C.'s persistence was rewarded as he became the school's most gifted musician. And no matter what his teachers taught, he continued to absorb all the jazz and blues music he could hold. "My ears were sponges," he recalled. "Soaked it all in." A big band leader named Artie Shaw inspired R. C. to learn the clarinet, and from there he branched into the saxophone and trumpet.

R. C. soon began to compose music, which he enjoyed as much as playing it. He became a fixture at school assemblies with such arrangements as "Jingle Bell Boogie," which he wrote for himself and five singers. Such programs could also lead to trouble, as when he once replaced a classical tune he was scheduled to play with the suggestive blues tune "Romance in the Dark." He was warned, in no uncertain terms, never to perform such a song again.

Still, R. C. found increasing opportunities to be heard, even outside of school. His music teacher arranged off-campus gigs at women's tea parties. He earned praise, good food, and sometimes even a few dollars for his efforts. R. C. was delighted at being paid for doing what made him happy and wondered how far his talent could take him.

R. C.'s musical achievements bolstered his confidence and determination not to be defeated by blindness. He strolled faster than most sighted people, learning navigational tricks such as distinguishing walls from open spaces by the way his footsteps echoed in a hallway. "I just do like a bat," he joked. During summer breaks, he amazed folks back home in Greenville by learning to ride a bicycle. As friends shouted directions, he raced around town with hardly a mishap.

By age fifteen, R. C. felt like he was on top of his world. He was a bright, if somewhat mischievous, student, a talented musician, and one of the most popular kids at his school. He was also totally unprepared for the jolt that came next. He was informed that his mother, Retha, had died. Her death was attributed to a food reaction, but nobody really knew the cause for sure since she received little medical attention. Retha was only thirty-one years old.

R. C. was numb with grief. "Nothing had ever hit me like that," he later declared. "Not George drowning. Not going blind. Nothing." After her funeral he fell into a tailspin. He stopped eating and sleeping for days until people began to worry that his own sorrow might land him beside his mother in the grave.

Finally, a respected elderly woman known throughout the black community as Ma Beck sat R. C. down. She told the forlorn blind teenager, "Your mama spent her whole life preparing you for this here day. . . . [Y]ou know what she told you. You gotta carry on. That's all there is to it. That's what she'd want. And that's what you gotta do."

Ma Beck's simple logic penetrated R. C.'s wall of denial. He knew she was right; his mother had devoted herself to training R. C. for a world without her. Never did he dream it would happen so soon, but now he had to accept her death and move on.

The loss continued to leave its mark on R. C. after he returned to school in the fall. Retha's death had matured her son quickly. He was more a young man than a boy, and campus routines and regulations now seemed babyish to him. Maybe, he figured, he had outgrown the school.

Meanwhile, music was calling R. C. louder than ever. He had been hired for gigs by jazz bands while visiting family friends in Jacksonville, at that time Florida's largest city. R. C. had become so sure of his talent that while rehearsing for a live radio broadcast, he informed the conductor of the studio orchestra that one of his violinists was flat. A school friend who accompanied R. C. to the station was incredulous that his black, teenaged friend would attempt to correct an older professional— and a white one at that. However, R. C. turned out to be correct.

Back at school, R. C. embarked on a string of minor pranks that soon landed him in the principal's office under threat of expulsion. He retorted that they couldn't expel him from school because he was quitting. The final entry in his student record was, "Sent home Oct. 5, 1945. Unsatisfactory pupil." With a dollar or two in his pocket, R. C. cast himself into a new world.

Challenged as he was by blindness, R. C. was determined to avoid stereotypes. He even turned down a charitable offer of a seeing-eye dog. "That was one of the three big NO's," he pointed out. "No dog, no cane, no guitar." He added the guitar taboo to his list because it seemed that every blind singer he heard was playing one.

Charles's registration card at the Florida School for the Deaf and the Blind.

Name _Robinson, R. C._	Registration No. _Blind-277-C_	
Date of Birth _Sept. 23, 1930_ Sex _Male_	Year	Supervisor
Date Admitted _October 23, 1937_ County _Madison_	_1942-1943_	_Ernest Lawrence_
Cause of Deafness or Blindness _Hereditary hues_	_1943-1944_	_Cary White_
Baptist	_1944-1945_	_Cary White_
Parents Name and Address _Reather Williams_ _Mrs. Mary Jane Robinson_ _Greenville, Florida_	_1945-1946_	_Cary White_
Sent home Oct. 5, 1945 _Unsatisfactory pupil_		

All R. C. really needed were his fingers. Music was his love, and also his only potential source of income. Mary Jane, the closest person left to him, bought R. C. a train ticket to Jacksonville, home of most of the bands and clubs in Florida. He spent the ride listening to the rhythm of the wheels on the rails. The forward thrust was more than just the train; it was the direction of his life.

Jammin'

Though R. C. had left the security of school for the shaky freedom of a big city, he was not entirely alone. He moved in with Fred and Lena Mae Thompson, family friends he had been visiting during his summers. Since getting his bearings in a new area was a must for him, the Thompsons escorted R. C. on get-acquainted walks through downtown Jacksonville. As always, he memorized paths using landmarks few others noticed, such as cracks in the sidewalk or sewer covers.

One of the first routes R. C. learned was the short stroll from the Thompsons' to Local 632, the "colored" branch of Jacksonville's Musicians Union. Like most unions, this was a group of people in the same profession who joined forces to try to improve their working conditions and income. He introduced himself as R. C.

Robinson and lied about his age to get permission to play in adult nightclubs. R. C. spent afternoons and evenings hanging around the union hall's piano, which was a professional and social hub for the musicians who took turns showing off their skills. Many veterans were suspicious of this new blind whiz kid who could copy their best licks and looked nowhere near the twenty-one years he claimed.

"And I could understand how they felt," Ray admitted. "They were right. Once I heard what they'd be putting down, I started running with it. Like a thief in the night. But I also let the cats know that I was ready, willing and able to boogie-woogie for my dinner. I wasn't proud. I might say to some guy, 'Say, man, I'll play, and if you don't like it, don't pay me.'"

A riverfront neighborhood in the city of Jacksonville, Florida, as it looked in the mid-1940s when Charles moved there after leaving the Florida School for the Deaf and the Blind. *(Library of Congress)*

Some began to take up his offer. Bit by bit, R. C. filled in for bands and combos needing a pianist for the night. He started at a couple of dollars a gig but soon was earning upwards of five dollars a night. The blind musician knew exactly what he made because he insisted on payment in singles so he couldn't be cheated.

Within six months, R. C. landed regular work in a sixteen-piece house orchestra at a nightclub called the Two Spot. The soaring horns and driving rhythm section reminded him of one of his radio favorites, the Count Basie Orchestra. The difference: anchoring a piano in the midst of this swinging music at the Two Spot was not the Count but young R. C. Robinson himself.

The Two Spot was Jacksonville's hottest club and a hangout for musicians. Another bandleader inquired whether R. C. might like to be featured on piano and vocals for a Florida tour he was assembling, and he didn't have to ask twice. Only a year after the schoolboy struck out on his own, he was touring as a star with a big band.

R. C.'s musical dream soon lost its luster. The veteran members of the ensemble resented the young upstart's star status. When the band headed for its first round of engagements in the Orlando area, its van lacked enough seats for all the musicians. As the junior member, R. C. had to ride the 150 miles from Jacksonville on a soda crate.

Worse yet, the flood of gigs the bandleader anticipated trickled dry after only a few weeks. It was R. C.'s first exposure to a harsh reality of the music business: optimism does not always mean work. The band broke up, and most of its members straggled back to Jackson-ville. R. C. was less willing to retrace his steps and instead weighed his options.

There was no logical reason *not* to return to Jackson-ville; it certainly was a safer place to be. R. C. had established a musical reputation there, while in Orlando he would be starting from measure one. If he stumbled onto hard times in Jacksonville, the Thompsons were there to catch him. They had never accepted any money for his room and board. Whenever R. C. was a few dollars ahead, he had repaid their kindness by slipping a sack of groceries into the kitchen while they were away.

Still, the teenager felt determined to assert his inde-pendence. Though the blind sixteen-year-old's self-reliance already amazed most people he knew, R. C. had not convinced his toughest critic: himself. Orlando seemed like a good proving ground. If he hit bottom there, nobody would automatically pick him up.

R. C.'s desire to be tested was granted with a ven-geance. Orlando in 1946 was hardly the booming city fueled by tourism that it became when Disney World opened twenty-five years later. It was still a sleepy town of 55,000 people, about 15,000 of them black. In the segregated South of that time, R. C. could play only at venues that accepted members of his race. Many local African Americans were seasonal pickers in the sur-rounding orange and grapefruit groves, with little en-ergy or change in their pockets at the end of the day. Orlando had few working bands, and more than enough

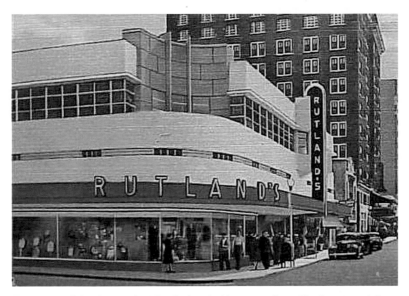

Downtown Orlando was just beginning to blossom when Charles moved there in 1946. This picture from a 1940s postcard shows the famous Rutland Building along Orlando's main drag, Orange Avenue.

musicians to fill their ranks. A union card made little difference there.

R. C.'s plucky spirit sometimes had to substitute for money. The landlady at his boardinghouse was lenient if he fell behind on his three-dollars-a-week rent. A. J. Kleckly, the owner of the Knick-Knack Café, remembered, "[R. C.] was a bouncy fellow, always a cheerful word for everybody: 'Hey, how you doing, what's up my friend?'" Kleckly was also amazed that although sightless, R. C. easily plugged the Knick-Knack's pay phone with nickels when making calls. Often, the likeable young man enjoyed a free meal.

Such kindnesses, though, were the exception, not the rule. Soon, food became as scarce for R. C. as performing gigs. Occasionally, he pooled his money with other struggling musicians for a bag of beans and a slab of fatback bacon, which they cooked together and considered a feast. Other times, when R. C. was flat broke and wearing out his welcome at the Knick-Knack, he didn't eat for a day or two. It was the most impoverished he had ever been; even in his darkest childhood days his stomach had usually been full. R. C. never forgot the gnawing of hunger and became even more determined to succeed.

When musicians in Orlando weren't working, they "jammed." Jam sessions were not only a way to practice but sort of a musical game of King of the Hill. Though most of the musicians were friends, songs became battlegrounds as instrumentalists tried to outplay each other. "You either cut the mustard or had the mustard smeared all over your sorry face," Ray recalled. His victories in many of these cutting contests leapfrogged him over others in the pecking order of available musicians.

What eventually lifted him over the top was his ability to arrange as well as perform music. The leader of the house band at the Sunshine Club, Orlando's biggest black nightspot, was thrilled to learn that R. C. could not only play but write arrangements of popular songs exclusively for his band. Typically, bandleaders had to buy charts for each instrument from a music publisher, but this talented and hungry young rookie was willing to do it for free. R. C. was thrilled merely to have a job and hear his arrangements being played. He even wrote his first original song, "Confession Blues," for the band to play.

As usual, R. C.'s blindness created some daunting challenges. He had to compose each instrument's part completely in his head, then dictate it note by note to another musician who wrote it down. By contrast, sighted arrangers usually compared parts to each other and revised them as they went along. R. C.'s band mates were amazed at how perhaps a dozen different parts he "wrote" without inspecting his work blended perfectly when performed together.

Flush with success and a bit of cash, R. C. spent would-be grocery money on his first record player. He bought dozens of fragile shellac records and never broke one. Buying his own records opened R. C.'s ears to music beyond hits on the radio and broadened his influences even more. His favorite pianist was Art Tatum, a jazz artist whose dazzling runs seemed to come from many more hands than two. Interestingly, Tatum was almost as blind as R. C. His collection also included the great vocalists Ella Fitzgerald and Billie Holiday, and player/arrangers such as saxophonist Benny Carter.

R. C. spotted an emerging trend in two of his favorite types of music. Newly popular blues musicians such as Muddy Waters and T-Bone Walker were electronically amplifying their guitars for a harder-driving sound. Boogie-woogie jazz pianists were also turning up the volume, and the fusion of these new sounds in the late 1940s became known as rhythm and blues, or R&B.

Of the new crop of popular artists, Nat "King" Cole made the greatest impression. Cole's smooth voice and textured piano fills were popular with both black and white audiences. His universal appeal was not lost on the youngster soaking up his records down in Florida.

Nathaniel Coles was four years old when he moved with his family from Alabama to Chicago's South Side. In 1923, the neighborhood was ablaze with the music of another migrant from the South, Louis Armstrong. The New Orleans native and his cornet were rapidly establishing jazz as the hottest music in the world, with Chicago as its epicenter.

By the 1930s, Armstrong had moved to New York, but Chicago was still a jazz hotbed that enticed the teenaged Coles. The boy became an organist in the church where his father preached, but spent most of his free time at jazz clubs, listening outside the door when he was too young to get inside. Coles's keyboard virtuosity soon convinced managers to ignore his underage status. The teenager was performing regularly and even recording by age seventeen.

Within a year, Coles took to the road with a musical revue. Like young R. C. Robinson ten years later, he itched to make a splash at a national level. When the revue suddenly folded in California, Coles decided to try his luck on the West Coast. A gimmick-minded nightclub owner put a paper crown on his head and nicknamed him King Cole, after the Old King Cole

Opposite: Charles's idol, Nat "King" Cole. *(Courtesy of Getty Images.)*

nursery rhyme.

The crown soon disappeared, but the name stuck. The King Cole Trio, with Nat "King" Cole at the helm, soon went on a national tour. Cole began singing and became even more popular. In 1943, the King Cole Trio signed with the newly formed Capitol Records. Within a year, they had a hit—"Straighten Up and Fly Right"—which Cole had written after recalling one of his father's sermons. Other successes, such as "Route 66," followed, and Cole's fame inspired young R. C., who was just launching his own musical journey.

To R. C., Cole defined cool. He was a black man who could connect with anyone and seemed immune to the prejudices directed at his race. In reality, Cole's suave exterior concealed inner turmoil that left him with bleeding ulcers and a three-pack-a-day smoking habit. In 1965, as the older Ray Charles confronted comparable pressures of his own, Cole died from lung cancer at just forty-five years old.

By then, Cole's influence had made R. C. aware that a black musician could have universal appeal. "I ate, slept and drank everything Nat King Cole," Ray confessed. "He became my idol."

His Cole impersonation paid off as R. C. began to gain local fame as a "little Nat." Combined with his youth, blindness, and undeniable talent, R. C. was hard to forget. His ego began to rise as steadily as his star, until one afternoon when he was abruptly jerked back to Earth.

The reality check was provided by Lucky Millinder, a top bandleader of the time. Millinder, who was a fixture at famous jazz havens such as New York's Cotton Club and the Savoy Ballroom, was playing Orlando's Sunshine Club for a weekend as part of a national tour. He was told about the blind

Lucky Millinder.

young local sensation and agreed to give him an audition. Millinder listened while R. C. regaled him with several songs. His simple verdict struck R. C. like a bolt of lightning: "Ain't good enough kid . . . you don't got what it takes."

He was cut to the bone, and the street-hardened teenager went straight home and cried like a baby. Millinder's rejection was a lesson in humility he would never forget. "At the time I thought Lucky was cold blooded," he explained, "but Lucky was just honest. I had potential, but in the '40s, jazz musicians were right on it; they didn't want to hear about no potential."

He practiced harder, focused on making the big time.

The first step in R. C.'s strategy was to leave Orlando, which had provided him more hunger than hope. At seventeen, he headed down the highway to the larger Florida city of Tampa.

Tampa was a bustling seaport with a larger market of people with money to spend. Many of them were sailors and dock workers from elsewhere, with a more open mind toward entertainers. The city was more progressive and R. C. could play at nightspots and events for black patrons and at many whites-only clubs. As he put it, "Nobody had to tell me that white people had the money."

R. C.'s "little Nat" routine was especially popular at white clubs. He quickly learned the songs people requested most often and was rewarded with large tips. People were drawn to the novelty of a blind teenager who could copy Cole note for note.

Branching out, R. C. landed a spot in a white "hillbilly" band, the Florida Playboys. Drawing upon his years of listening to the Grand Ole Opry, the black pianist sang country songs and even learned to yodel. If white audiences were initially uneasy with his color, R. C.'s blindness shielded him from their scowls. In the end, his talent always won them over.

Among the many musicians R. C. met in Tampa was a friendly young guitarist named Gossie McKee. McKee was as footloose and ambitious as R. C. He had played up north and told his fellow black musician about the more equal treatment there. In northern cities R. C.

wouldn't be driven away from restaurants or public bathrooms, McKee assured him. Why shouldn't they go north, where they could play anywhere and live freely?

It was a tempting proposition. R. C. was often making decent money in Tampa: fifteen to twenty dollars a gig with the Florida Playboys and up to thirty dollars in tips on evenings he performed his Nat Cole routine with a quartet. Still, he frequently played roadhouses so rough he memorized the path to the nearest window so he could escape if a vicious fight erupted. Plus, it seemed that no big-name musicians lived in Florida. Everyone who was anyone was from somewhere else.

The two young men pulled out a map, determined to find the farthest big city from Florida. They settled on Seattle, Washington, even though neither had ever set foot in their destination over 3,000 miles away. When the time came to leave, R. C. hesitated, caught up in a new romance. He was head-over-heels in love with a pretty young girl, Louise Mitchell. They had even taken an apartment together—despite her parents' objections. R. C. instructed McKee to go ahead to Seattle and said that he would follow soon. His friend was no fool. McKee guaranteed the arrangement by taking something R. C. could not live without: his records.

Sure enough, within a couple of weeks, R. C. parted with his girlfriend and boarded a bus to Seattle. The five-day trip seemed to take forever. Tucked into the back section, where blacks were still expected to sit, and nibbling crackers and candy bars, R. C. looked every bit the part of a helpless, blind black man with no apparent means of support. Nobody knew that hidden in his bag was $500 he had saved from musical earnings, which he would stake on a shot at fame in Seattle.

Chitlin Circuit

4

Since R. C.'s bus rolled into Seattle in the middle of the night, the first thing he did was get a good day's sleep. Then, almost immediately, he landed a job.

Gossie McKee had booked his weary friend a room in the hotel where he was staying. When R. C. awoke that evening, McKee laid out a plan. He had lined up a chance for the two of them to play a set a few hours later at a nightclub called the Black and Tan.

And play they did. R. C. reported years later that he tore through several songs he knew "as well as my own mother, and when I'm through, I can tell the folks dig it. The place rings with applause." By the end of their set, the pair had lined up gigs not only at the Black and Tan but at spots such as the Seattle Elks Club.

After almost starving in Florida a little over a year

The booming city of Seattle, Washington, in the mid-1940s.

earlier, R. C. couldn't believe his good fortune. The city they picked off a map was a winner, at least for musicians. Tampa may have been bustling, but Seattle was an outright boomtown. The West Coast port enjoyed a brisk economy fueled by international trade and aircraft factories that mushroomed during World War II. Fort Lewis, one of the nation's largest military bases, also loomed over Seattle during and after the conflict. At war's end, the base housed thousands of soldiers with plenty of money in their pockets, who cruised Seattle's freewheeling Jackson Street for entertainment in their spare time. As one musician from the period remembered, "They did everything but go home."

Nat "King" Cole was becoming more popular than ever, and so was R. C.'s imitation of him. He had also expanded his performance with an impersonation of

Charles Brown, another R&B artist catching fire nationally. Brown sang in a more raw, bluesy style well suited to R. C.'s singing voice. For the time being, he had no qualms about imitating these famous singers.

"Someone asked me if I felt bad being a copycat for so long," he once admitted. "'Feel bad?' I said. 'Honey, I feel *good* any time I can make good money making good music!'"

R. C. and guitarist McKee added a bass player to exactly match the lineup of Cole's and Brown's trios. Now they needed a name. The original members combined their names—Gossie McKee and R. C. Robinson— and the McSon Trio was born.

In 1944, Seattle had over two dozen busy clubs, and the McSon Trio played most of them. Some nights they began the evening with a country club dinner, followed by a couple of hours at a nightclub, and ending with their regular after-midnight gig at the Rocking Horse. With tips, the band could net over one hundred dollars in an evening, a fortune for most musicians back then.

R. C. had lived what seemed like an entire life by age eighteen, but suddenly, at least among music lovers, he was the toast of his newly adopted town. The McSon Trio played on local radio and became the first black people to appear on Seattle's new television station. The band bought chic matching double-breasted suits and issued a publicity photo.

About this time, McKee noticed that some people were uncomfortable about R. C.'s missing eye. He sug-

This is the first known picture of Ray Charles, taken in Seattle in 1948.

gested that the blind pianist wear sunglasses when he played. The dark glasses bolstered R. C.'s cool image and would become the best-known item in his wardrobe.

Among the multitude drawn to Seattle's new sensation was a black high school student named Quincy Jones. Jones, like R. C. during his student days in Florida, was considered a musical prodigy who loved jazz and could write arrangements as well as play them on his trumpet. R. C. took a liking to the earnest teenager only a couple of years his junior, while Jones was awed by the worldliness that seemed to radiate from his mentor, who like him, had endured poverty and a broken family.

"Ray Charles was a man," Jones attested. "He had his own apartment, his own record player, his own older girlfriend, three suits, his own

Quincy Jones in the 1940s.

life. That's something I wanted more than anything else." Jones sought help with his arrangements, which R. C. was happy to provide. They spent hours dissecting charts at the McSon star's house, often noodling out tunes on the electric piano R. C. had purchased shortly after the instrument went on the market. The two young arrangers forged a friendship that would span decades and continents.

The female companion Jones envied was R. C.'s Tampa sweetheart Louise, who had moved to Seattle to be with him. Though they were in love, the pressures of setting up a household while still in their teens created a turbulent relationship. Within a year, they had broken up, and Louise headed back to her parents in Florida.

The house in which Charles and his girlfriend Louise lived on 24th Avenue in Seattle before Louise returned home to Florida.

When Louise arrived home, she realized she was pregnant. The young couple agreed that she should have the baby. Perhaps they might still get back together. As it turned out, the prospective reunion never happened. In what became a pattern over his life, R. C. sent money when he could to help support the child of a woman he never married.

In Seattle, R. C. fell into another habit that would dog him for years. Many of the older musicians he played with took drugs. Though they tried to discourage the teenager, R. C. was soon smoking marijuana and wanting more. He longed to try heroin, which was fast becoming the drug of choice among the hipsters of the jazz world. Ray believed that heroin improved the ability of well-known users such as jazz singer Billie Holiday and the famous saxophonist Charlie Parker to feel their music.

Heroin is classified as an opiate, one of the many drugs derived from poppy flowers. Opiates are mainly used as pain relievers and sleep inducers. The hold heroin had over so many talented musicians and artists of the era can be attributed to many different factors, the most basic of which was its powerful addictive qualities. Because stars like Holiday and Parker were so dependant on the drug, it came to be seen as the source of their musical powers, rather than something that was slowly draining those powers away. Much of heroin's cachet came from its association with those famous figures, and new users only needed a few experiences before they, too, were hooked.

Within another decade, Holiday and Parker were dead from heroin overdoses, but for now R. C. was enamored with the myth of heroin as a self-starter for creative juices. Veteran jazz junkies warned him to steer clear of the drug, but R. C. wasn't in a mood to listen. He began injecting heroin and was soon addicted.

For now, though, the most exciting development was that the McSon Trio was gaining notice throughout the musical grapevine all the way down the West Coast. One night, a black man from Los Angeles introduced himself during the band's break at the Rocking Horse. He was Jack Lauderdale, and he owned a label called Down Beat

The McSon Trio in 1948: Ray on piano, Gossie McKee on guitar, and Milton Garred on bass.

Records. He liked their sound and wondered if the trio would like to cut a record.

R. C. tried to appear casual, but he didn't have to be asked twice. "Good God almighty!" he thought. "Just show us the way, Papa. Nothing I want to do more"—cut a record, just like the ones he used to spin on Mr. Pit's jukebox, but with his name on it. To commemorate this career milestone, R. C. Robinson decided to change his name to something more memorable: Ray Charles.

The trio cut their record the very next day in a small

Ray's first record, "Confession Blues."

Seattle studio Lauderdale had rented. The opening selection was the first song Charles had written back in Florida, "Confession Blues." He sang it in his Charles Brown style. To cover himself, Charles recorded a song for the flip side in his Nat Cole voice.

They recorded each song to Lauderdale's liking after one try. The music executive they hardly knew told them not to worry about a contract, that they could work it out later. The happy but naïve musicians didn't care. The truth was that they would have cut a record for free just to hear it played.

"Confession Blues" got more radio play of the two sides. *Billboard* magazine rated record popularity by sales, as it still does today. "Confession Blues" peaked at number five on the race records chart, which at that time included most black recordings. The three young men who cut it were ecstatic. When their name was accidentally printed as the Maxin Trio on the record label, they quickly changed from the McSon Trio to match the mistake.

Down Beat's Lauderdale was pleased as well. Within a year, he sent an invitation to record at his home studio in Los Angeles. He included fifty dollars, but only two plane tickets. Bassist Milton Garred was not invited. Then McKee received a jolt once he arrived in the studio. Lauderdale had brought in a guitarist he liked better to handle lead parts, and the McSon Trio's co-founder was bumped to playing chords in the background.

It was clear that the real reason for the session was "The Blind Piano Sensation, Ray Charles," as Lauderdale soon promoted him. Still, Down Beat Records' aspiring star was a sensation without a salary. After cutting six sides, Charles and McKee didn't receive any plane tickets back to Seattle. Lauderdale finally bought them a broken-down used car without a heater so they could sputter home.

It didn't matter because within six months Lauderdale talked Charles into quitting the trio and moving to Los Angeles for good. Two years in Seattle had served the young pianist well, but like a talented baseball player, he was ready for a major league opportunity. By

1950, Los Angeles fit the bill. The California metropolis had exploded in growth in the past couple of decades to become the nation's third largest city. Both Nat Cole and Charles Brown shot to national fame from Los Angeles, a fact that was not lost on their young imitator. The movie industry was centered in Hollywood as well, creating an additional hunger for melodies that put L.A. on the short list of top musical centers.

Charles's debut session in L.A. reflected his growing status as a recording artist. Backing him this time were eight musicians, the largest ensemble he had played with since his big band days in Florida. Plus, in an unprecedented gesture, Lauderdale paid Charles over eighty dollars on the day of the recording.

This show of support gave the young man a relaxed confidence, and he began to ease away from his Cole and Brown imitations toward a style that was more uniquely Ray Charles. He punctuated a song called "I'll Do Anything for You" with the laughing comeback: ". . . but work!" Charles would later make a habit of talking as well as singing during his recordings, for a more personal delivery.

The session yielded no hits, so he tried again in a few more months. Among the new results was a catchy tune called "Baby Let Me Hold Your Hand." Thinking of his electric piano at home, Charles opened the song playing the celeste, an unusual keyboard that is connected to bells for a playful, tinkling effect. "Baby" made the *Billboard* charts and was his best seller to date.

The biggest star in Lauderdale's recording stable was a blues singer and guitarist named Lowell Fulson (he also recorded under the name Fulsom). The record executive had an idea: how about sending them together on a national tour? Charles wasn't yet enough of a name to draw big crowds himself, but he could gain exposure through a featured spot in Fulson's band. Each show included a segment where Fulson stepped away from his microphone, and Charles sang a few songs. The star, in turn, received a top-notch musician who would improve his sound. Everybody won.

An advertisement for one of Charles's appearances with Lowell Fulson. (Schomburg Center)

The tour launched in June 1950, rolling east on the same Route 66 immortalized in Nat Cole's hit song. In the pecking order of the star system, Fulson was chauffeured in a large Buick, while the rest of the band crammed into a station wagon. Charles didn't care; he received $35 a show and, more importantly, the chance to tour nationally. Not bad for a blind musician who had not yet turned twenty.

As a race records artist known mostly among black people, Fulson was denied the swankier ballrooms and auditoriums reserved for entertainers popular with white audiences. Fulson and his all-black peers played dances and nightclubs in sections of cities populated by African Americans. At the upper end were a few venues such as Harlem's Apollo Theater, a black institution that launched the careers of superstars such as Ella Fitzgerald and, in

RACE RECORDS: MUSIC FOR ALL

If the first years of the recording industry could be painted in a color, it would be white. From the phonograph's invention in 1877, hardly any black performers were captured on the disks that became known as records. Then, in 1920, Okeh Records released a recording called "Crazy Blues" by a black cabaret singer named Mamie Smith. It sold over two million copies, and record companies suddenly realized the market potential of 14 million black Americans.

Early black recordings were marketed as race records and usually separated from those made by white artists. Okeh set up its Original Race Records division in 1921, and other major labels such as Columbia and Victor soon followed suit. Except for a few labels such as Black Swan, blacks recorded as race record artists for white-owned companies.

Most race records were sold in black neighborhoods to buyers such as Mr. Pit, whose jukebox had enthralled Ray Charles as a boy. Establishments frequented by African Americans pulsed with these "gut bucket" blues, songs named for the marinated hog intestines often consumed where the disks played. And there they usually stayed because record executives considered music such as blues and gospel too primitive to engage white audiences.

In time some black artists, like jazzman Louis Armstrong, who cut his first records as an Okeh race musician, would break through the color barrier to wide popularity across racial lines. More often, black artists were popular mainly with black people. White record executives had no problem with this as long as those artists could sell millions of records to black Americans.

By the time Charles recorded, small independent or "indie" labels were moving into the race records arena. Many, such as Swing Time, were black-owned. A few were run by whites who liked black music. Charles's second record label, Atlantic, was managed by an unlikely trio: Ahmet Ertegun, a Turkish immigrant; Herb Abramson, a dentist; and a music journalist, Jerry Wexler. A former writer for *Billboard* magazine, Wexler first called race music "rhythm and blues" in 1949, and the term stuck through the 1950s and beyond.

Most race record companies, including Black Swan and, later, Swingtime, flourished for a few years before going under. Atlantic was an exception. As rhythm and blues bridged into white-fueled rock and roll—and changed popular music forever—Atlantic enjoyed success with Charles and eventually artists as diverse as soul singer Aretha Franklin and British rockers Led Zeppelin. Though today records are produced by huge companies for all races, one-time musical maverick Atlantic still exists, now as a major label.

later years, Michael Jackson. More typical were the likes of tobacco warehouse "ballrooms" in Southern states, where dancers kicked up dust that choked the band by evening's end.

In the South, Charles was reintroduced to the segregated society he had fled when he left Florida. He had encountered racial barriers in the North, but not like this. Fortunately, Charles couldn't see the "No Dogs or

Niggers Allowed" signs that sometimes greeted the band at restaurants. Still, he shared their hunger when they were refused service, and the humiliation of having to use the woods instead of a whites-only restroom. Years later, when the civil rights movement demolished segregation across the U.S., Charles recalled, "It's detestable when you live it."

In Myrtle Beach, South Carolina, Charles learned that even water can be segregated. He was enjoying a swim in the ocean when a band mate began screaming at him. Figuring he had wandered out too far, he paddled back toward the yelling comrade he could hear but not see. The man breathlessly informed Charles that he had almost swam over to the white side, which would have meant big trouble.

"*White side!*" Charles marveled. "Who ever knew of such a thing? I couldn't figure out how the ocean could have a white side and a black side. It struck me as being funny: not funny-funny, but funny-ridiculous, funny-sad."

Discrimination did occasionally work to the band's benefit. At places where they were turned away from white-run hotels and restaurants, they roomed at boardinghouses and ate at diners owned by blacks. Such services were often cheaper, and Charles found that he could save $10-15 a day after his expenses.

This was fortunate because, like many up-and-coming young musicians on small labels, he had not received a dime from Jack Lauderdale for his record sales.

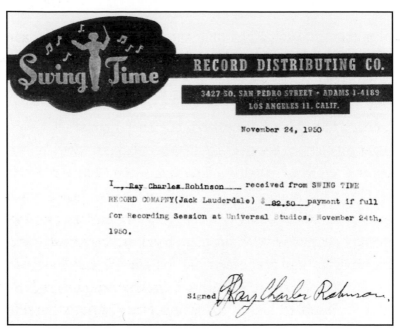

A receipt signed by Ray Charles for a recording session with Jack Lauderdale's studio.

Charles learned other ways to be paid, such as feeding his boss's reputation as a high roller at the gambling halls he frequented. "I said, 'Hey Jack, let me have $500, I want to get into the game,'" Charles explained. "And I'd say it in front of everyone, so he would. I'd bet a hundred and keep the other four."

As he became accustomed to life on the road, Charles continued to struggle in other areas of his life. A friend's girlfriend introduced him to a hairdresser, Eileen Williams, who soon began accompanying him on tour. When the couple that brought them together was married, Charles and Eileen followed suit four days later, seeking out a justice of the peace for a quick ceremony. But the hasty decision was one they would regret. Eileen eventually grew tired of life on the road, and Charles was too happy touring to settle down with her. They parted ways and would soon finalize the end of their relationship with an official divorce.

By 1952, Charles sensed the same type of restlessness he eventually felt during his stints in Florida and Seattle. Granted, life could be worse. Fulson's band was playing classier venues, and Charles's salary had nudged up to fifty dollars a show. He used his increased earnings to buy his own car and hire a driver so he could travel more comfortably.

Still, Charles wondered whether his career had stalled. Down Beat Records had changed its name to Swing Time, but little else. Charles's new records continued to sell modestly, and he still received no royalties. Just as he was pondering his chances with another record company, Lauderdale made the decision easier. Strapped for cash, the man who had approached Charles in Seattle three years earlier full of high hopes suddenly exercised his option to sell Charles's contract to another record company. He spun off his onetime sensation for $2,500.

Charles got the news that his new home would be Atlantic Records in New York, a label he had never heard of before. On one hand, he was grateful for a fresh start. On the other, he was beginning to realize that talent was only one factor in the mix of musical success. Would he be able to make the right records, heard by the right people? These questions weighed on his mind as he traveled to New York for his first session with Atlantic.

Hallelujah! The Big Time

5

In September 1952, Charles navigated the bustling streets of New York's Manhattan with two things on his mind. One was finding Atlantic Records' headquarters at 234 56th Street. Already a veteran of locating places he couldn't see in strange towns, Charles had to remember data such as addresses or other identifiers precisely so he could ask for help or relay information to a cab driver. He remembered this one by how the numbers lined up: 2-3-4-5-6.

Beyond that, Charles wondered what Atlantic owners Ahmet Ertegun and Herb Abramson would expect from him. He had borrowed a score of musical styles ranging from Cole- and Brown-like vocals to Count Basie piano riffs; what would his new bosses want him to play? Their answer—anything he wanted—was a breath of fresh air.

The skyline of Manhattan in 1952. *(Library of Congress)*

Atlantic's approach was to sign promising artists for the growing R&B market and let them loose. This wisdom had paid off with three number-one R&B hits in the company's four-year history from budding stars such as Ruth Brown and Big Joe Turner. Atlantic had similarly great expectations for the blind piano sensation. "I thought Ray Charles was about the best artist I'd ever heard that we had a chance to sign," Ertegun said.

The owners encouraged Charles not just to play what moved him but to write his own material as well. The result was four songs, including three originals, that were sung and played in a hodgepodge of styles and went nowhere when released as singles. Three more sessions over the next year produced some great music but nothing that scored on the charts.

Atlantic's hot young prospect was beginning to question his course. He had not released anything lately that outsold his original Down Beat hit, "Confession Blues." By comparison, other Atlantic artists had charted three top ten hits on *Billboard's* R&B chart during 1952, and the next year label newcomer Clyde McPhatter shot to number one on his first try with "Money Honey." Jerry Wexler, who had just left *Billboard* magazine to produce records for Atlantic, was reassuring. He told Charles, "We'll take care of the marketing. You just keep making the music; the hits will come."

Jerry Wexler *(left)* and Ahmet Ertegun *(middle)* are photographed with an unidentified woman at the Atlantic Records offices in 1952. Promotional posters for some of Atlantic's musicians hang on the wall above. *(Courtesy of Getty Images.)*

Buoyed by this support, the determined young man made a life-changing decision: "[S]top this Nat Cole imitation; sink, swim or die. I owe something to Ray first," he vowed. "I can't bull me." In the studio and on the bandstand, Charles opened his voice to a range of sounds, from screams to whispers, that were all his own.

Sounding good on tour was important because, for one thing, it increased exposure for his recordings. Plus, it was still his major source of income. Atlantic was fair about paying Charles the royalties due to him, but his record sales were hardly stunning. He was still touring either as a featured artist behind better-known performers, as he had with Lowell Fulson, or as a soloist accompanied by a pickup band of hastily assembled local musicians in cities where he played. The results from these haphazard unions could be painful.

Finally, during a weeklong stint in Philadelphia in 1954 with another thrown-together combo, Charles moaned, "The cats were so off that they literally hurt my ears. Man, I love music and I hate to hear it wrong. The band was so bad I went back to my hotel and cried." He gave his booking manager an ultimatum: if he kept touring, it had to be with his own band.

It was a bold move for a twenty-three-year-old with no big hit to his name, but it worked. Charles's handlers worked out a compromise solution. Ruth Brown, one of Atlantic's hottest stars of the moment, needed a band for a two-week tour. Charles would put together a group that would be used in full sets backing both artists. If it worked, Charles could continue with his own band after the tour with Brown was over.

Charles put together a seven-piece band of the hottest musicians he could find, and the tour was a success. He got to keep his band, but with it came the responsibility of meeting its expenses. His take became whatever was left after the band had been paid. Keeping the band afloat meant generating more income. Though Atlantic's management was willing to be patient, the band now gave Charles another reason why he needed a hit.

With his new ensemble, Charles toured harder than ever. When they weren't playing, the band spent hours driving to gigs in their two cars. The road could be a friend and an enemy—long road trips sometimes meant missed jobs. There was another factor menacing the band's success: Charles's growing heroin addiction. Though the musicians quickly came to realize that Charles was demanding on stage, they respected his talent and worked hard to meet his expectations. Offstage, however, they were disappointed to see their leader disappear behind locked doors with his dealer. Heroin became a kind of silent presence that divided band members into two camps: those that understood its language and those that did not. Restless hours on the road fostered more tension.

The car radio was the band's constant companion. Charles frequently tuned in to religious stations broadcasting the same type of gospel music he had loved as a child. One night while rolling through Indiana, Charles and his trumpet player began spicing up a song on the radio with lyrics that would never be heard in church: "I got a woman, way across town, she's good to me . . ." By morning they had a new song, "I Got a Woman," which married their own jumping, gospel-like melody to very secular lyrics.

With a score Charles wrote for the band, they tried "I Got a Woman" and other new material on crowds as their tour swung south. Audiences loved it, and Charles asked Atlantic's Ertegun and Wexler if they could set up a recording session while he was on the road. Everyone met in Atlanta, where Charles and the band cut several new songs they'd been playing on tour.

"I Got a Woman" blew the Atlantic executives away with what Wexler called "the blasphemous idea of taking gospel songs and putting the devil's words to them." In 1955, it peaked at number two on *Billboard's* R&B chart.

It took thirty months for Ray to have a hit with Atlantic, but the timing was fortunate. That year, a new form of rhythmic teenage music called rock and roll went over the top with the emergence of a white, swivel-hipped singer named Elvis Presley. Rock and roll not only straddled the racial fence, it struck a responsive chord among teenagers who chafed under a conservative American environment in the post-World War II years. Rock and roll was *their* music, and when parents criticized it, the kids loved it even more.

Presley and other early white rock and rollers borrowed heavily from black R&B artists; Elvis himself immediately put "I Got a Woman" into his own act. And while many black artists felt ripped off, some R&B masters such as Fats Domino, Chuck Berry, and Little Richard were able to break through the old race records barrier to sell their music in the lucrative white market. Having just scored a hit on *Billboard's* R&B chart, Charles now longingly eyed the Top 100 ranking of all popular, or pop, songs.

Charles has often been cited as one of the greatest influences on rock and roll, but he never felt he deserved the credit. His style was forged from a complex blend of jazz, blues, and gospel, unlike the stripped-down, beat-driven tunes and lyrics aimed directly at youngsters and performed by his R&B contemporaries Chuck Berry and Little Richard. "There's a towering difference between their music and mine," Ray said. "It was more difficult for teenagers to relate to, so much of my music was sad or down."

Berry and Little Richard enjoyed crossover success a year before Charles dented the pop charts. Perhaps Charles's greatest contribution to rock and roll was his influence on aspiring young musicians. A group of British teenagers who idolized Ray Charles eventually called themselves the Beatles and became the most successful chart-toppers of all time.

In the meantime, Charles's fusion of jazz, gospel, and R&B, driven by his unmistakable voice, left his fans— including his bosses at Atlantic—in awe. They began

ROCK, ROLL AND RAY

In 1952, a week after young Ray Charles played a concert at a Cleveland theater, local disc jockey Alan "Moondog" Freed hosted an event there that would make music history. Freed's Moondog Coronation Ball was something he called a "rock and roll party," after a phrase from one of the R&B songs he played on his radio show. He knew that both white and black teenagers listened to his show but was stunned when thousands from both races crashed the gates at the overfilled theater, causing the live performances—all black R&B acts—to be cancelled.

It was the first rock-and-roll riot, and it lit a fire for this music that would rage nationwide within a few years. Though it exploded most loudly in the gyrations of a white former truck driver from Memphis named Elvis Presley, rock and roll was fueled by black R&B artists who had labored on the Chitlin Circuit for years. Some early rock-and-roll hits were sanitized, white-sung covers of black R&B songs, but soon teenagers clamored for the real thing—and musicians like Charles were happy to deliver.

If history is the judge of rock-and-roll greatness, the verdict on Ray Charles was reached in 1986 at the opening of the Rock and Roll Hall of Fame in Cleveland, over thirty years after Freed's Moondog Coronation Ball. Out of hundreds of worthy candidates, ten were voted by ballot to be the first Hall of Fame members. The children of murdered Beatle John Lennon officially inducted one of those pioneer honorees: Ray Charles.

calling him "The Genius." "His whole approach to music has elements of genius in it, his concept of music is very different than anybody else's," Ertegun marveled.

A 1954 publicity shot of Charles for Atlantic Records.

As for Charles, he was well aware that, at least at first, his blend of church and juke joint music was not for everyone. "I got criticism from the churches, and from musicians too," he pointed out. "They thought it was sacrilegious or something, and what I was doing, I must be crazy. But I kept doing it, and eventually, instead of criticizing me for it, the people started saying I was an innovator. It's like a manager who makes a decision. If it works, he's a genius, and if it doesn't, he's an ass. What we did worked. So I became a genius for it."

Charles continued on his gospel-tinged trail, recording with three female singers who called themselves the Cookies, using the classic call-and-response technique he first heard in Florida churches as a child. In gospel music, a lead singer frequently calls a statement answered by a response from a chorus of voices. With Ray as "preacher," the sound would have fit comfortably into a black church—except he beckoned not to God but to a woman who had left him.

The formula spelled heaven to black listeners and provided Ray his first number one song on R&B charts in 1956 with "Drown in My Own Tears." A happier gospel-tinged song called "Hallelujah, I Love Her So" was a follow-up hit and garnered some airplay on the white-oriented rock-and-roll stations that had sprung up across America. The Cookies became the Raeletts and, shimmering in matching sequined gowns, joined Charles's expanding touring entourage.

Though Charles's restlessness and longing for the good life of the road helped make him a great musician, there was still a part of him that longed for stability and a real home. In 1955, he married for the second time. Della Beatrice Howard, known to all as Della Bea, was a member of a gospel singing group Charles admired. She came from a stable, middle-class family and, with her happy disposition and polite manners, seemed the opposite of the women Charles knew on the road. Della

The four original Raeletts in 1958 *(from left to right):* Ethel (Darlene) McRae, Gwen Berry, Pat Lyles, and Margie Hendricks. *(Michael Ochs Archives, Venice, California)*

Bea wanted a home and a family, and when she found herself pregnant with their first child, she insisted to Ray that one would not come without the other.

In March of 1955, Charles arrived in Dallas to meet Della Bea, then seven months pregnant. She picked out a house, he put down the rent, and they were married at the beginning of April. A few weeks later, he was back on the road.

Some of the things that came with being Mrs. Ray Charles were unpleasant. Ray was up front with Della Bea about his girlfriends, asking her to respect his privacy. She soon realized he was a drug user, too, but she kept her end of the bargain. In return, Ray did his best to keep his road life away from his home life. Over the years, Della Bea would give her husband three sons. She would keep their home, cook their food, and raise them while their father went out on the road. It would be an uneasy marriage, but Della tried hard to make it work.

Over the next two years, Charles's band rose to the top of the so-called Chitlin Circuit—the informal name given to the rounds of black nightclubs and restaurants. He bought a new type of vehicle made from a cut-in-half Chevrolet augmented by a six-foot passenger section in the middle. This forerunner of stretch limousines, promptly dubbed the "Weenie" by the band, carried all the musicians. It also lugged their instruments, including an electric piano Charles began taking on the road because he was sick of the out-of-tune instruments provided at venues. Even though some serious musicians considered the wired keyboard little more than a toy, it delivered a distinctive sound that helped differentiate Ray's style.

Since the band traveled almost constantly, they became a family of musical road warriors. Many whiled away their time playing a dice game called "four-five-six" that often lured Charles out of his chauffeured Cadillac to add his delighted howls to the merriment in the Weenie. He laughed, squealed, and slapped his thighs with delight as he fingered the dimples on the dice after each roll.

Onstage, Charles showed audiences this ecstatic side as well as genuine tears trickling from under his dark glasses, depending on how a song moved him. "Crying's always been a way for me to get things out which are buried deep, deep down," he once explained. "When I sing, I often cry. Crying is feeling, and feeling is being human."

Charles couldn't see his audiences, but band members informed him about the white youngsters who occasionally appeared. When Elvis recorded "I Got a Woman," Charles earned his biggest royalty check ever, just for having written the song. Clearly, crossover success as a performer among both black and white audiences would lift Charles's star—and his checkbook—to a new level.

As usual, Ray Charles was determined to follow his own unpredictable path. He updated an old song from the 1800s into the rollicking "Swanee River Rock." To his surprise, it broke onto *Billboard's* coveted Top 100 pop chart, peaking at number thirty-four. This first-ever musical venture onto the white side fared much better than his near-disastrous swim at Myrtle Beach a few years earlier.

At the other side of the musical scale, Atlantic executives encouraged their genius to flaunt the jazz piano skills that were being overshadowed by his soulful vocals. Ertegun and Wexler felt they had the perfect place to showcase Charles's jazz work: an emerging recording concept called an album. Records had always been released as singles with front and back sides, but a new technology enabled several songs to be pressed onto one larger disc.

The result was *The Great Ray Charles*, ten tracks of Charles playing piano and sax but not sing-

The cover of *The Great Ray Charles*.

ing. He was accompanied by highly respected jazz players, and his old Seattle friend Quincy Jones helped with arrangements. The album attracted enough sales and airplay on jazz stations to earn Charles an invitation to play at New York's famous Carnegie Hall, where classical rhapsodies were more common than rhythm and blues. The rising young musician was starstruck, playing a jazz concert in one of the world's premier halls, in a lineup topped by the aging but still-legendary Billie Holiday.

Carnegie Hall was prestigious and a far cry from Charles's typical venues. His band still labored in the trenches of smaller theaters and dance halls across the U.S., with a steadily growing following among both black and white teenagers and young adults. Charles's music was more complex than the three-chord guitar-driven rock pumped out by chart-toppers such as Elvis and Chuck Berry. And there was something about a Ray Charles performance that made it impossible to sit still.

By 1958, Charles's band often played five nights a week, and the Weenie often had to rush them to a different town every day. Back home, Della Bea had just given birth to her second son. Ray Charles Jr. was nearly three, and now the baby, David, joined the family. Ray saw them when he could, but he always went back to the road and his girlfriends. The life was hard, but he could not give it up. Many gigs were four-hour dances that Charles scrambled to fill with songs. Excitement rose to a fever pitch near the end, as dancers demanded one up-tempo tune after another.

At a one-nighter in Brownsville, Pennsylvania, Charles literally ran out of fast songs with fifteen minutes still remaining in his gig. He didn't want to send the crazed crowd home with slow ballads so he tried an experiment. Charles never forgot the evening that changed his life: "I said to the band and the Raeletts, 'Listen, I'm going to fool around and y'all just follow me.'" On his electric piano Ray began noodling a staccato riff that had just popped into his head. Then he added impromptu verses:

> Hey mama don't you treat me wrong,
> come and love your daddy all night long, hey, hey!
> See the girl with the diamond ring,
> she knows how to shake that thing, hey hey!
> Tell me what'd I say?

Opposite: Ray Charles performing at Carnegie Hall. *(Courtesy of Getty Images.)*

At that point the Raeletts chimed back "what'd I say" in the same call-and-response style they used on some of Charles's records. The crowd went crazy, and soon everyone in the audience was shouting back whatever the supercharged pianist sang. When Charles couldn't invent any more lyrics, he made noises that the dancers thundered back to him.

When the show finally ended, sweaty dancers rushed to the bandstand asking where they could buy a record of that song. Charles told them it hadn't been recorded but vowed to himself that it would be soon. Over the next several evenings the band refined "What'd I Say" and used it to end their gigs. Each night the result was the same, and Charles, who wasn't prone to bragging, phoned Ertegun and Wexler that he might have a hit on his hands.

In the studio, Charles, the Raeletts, and the band tried to capture the spontaneous excitement of their live performance, complete with shouts, groans, and pleadings not to stop. "What'd I Say" stretched on for several minutes, just like it did on stage. Atlantic faced a problem because most songs played on pop stations were no more than a few minutes long. The final edit of "What'd I Say" was over six minutes, so producers chopped it into "Part I" and "Part II" to fit neatly onto radio playlists.

Both pop and R&B stations embraced "What'd I Say" as soon as it was released in 1959. Amazingly, they usually played both sides together, in effect giving Charles twice the normal airtime an artist received. Listeners sang along with Charles over the radio, just as they did at his gigs, and bought the record in droves. "What'd I Say" was another number one R&B hit, but more importantly, it soared to number six on the lucrative pop charts. Ray Charles had finally arrived as a crossover artist.

The sky now seemed the limit for Atlantic's twenty-eight-year-old genius. Ertegun and Wexler eagerly wondered what surprises he would produce next.

The Hits
Keep Coming

6

Charles's next move was hardly what Ertegun and Wexler had anticipated: he switched record labels.

It wasn't something he had planned. His Atlantic contract was due for renewal, and he had every reason to remain with the company. Ertegun and Wexler treated him like a king; they had just run a full-page ad in *Billboard* promoting his latest album, *The Genius of Ray Charles.*

In the end, though, money shouted the loudest to a musician who had climbed out of the black hole of poverty. Charles was suddenly a very hot property and he was approached in late 1959 by a new record label: ABC. Unlike the independent Atlantic, ABC was created by a large corporation that included the ABC television network and a nationwide movie-house chain. Executives there offered him a larger royalty rate on record sales, guaranteed annual income, and sweetened the deal with a perk designed to grab Charles's attention.

ABC proposed to let Charles be producer—the general overseer—of all his recordings. As such, he would receive more money each time he went into the studio. Producing is a very important job; at Atlantic, Ertegun and Wexler, at least officially, performed this function on all of Charles's recordings. ABC had heard that Charles was an extremely competent, self-assured musician who had been totally in charge of recordings like "What'd I Say." Even Atlantic's Wexler admitted, "He had the total sound. We were the students, he was the teacher. We merely turned on the lights—which he didn't even need."

By permitting Charles to produce his own records, ABC was making a deal that, after a record made back its expenses, would pay Ray Charles seventy-five cents for every dollar of profit. The object of all this attention calmly listened to their generous offer, then floated his own request back across the table: as producer, he wanted to own his recording masters.

He couldn't see their stunned expressions, but the stony silence betrayed their shock. Masters were the final versions of recordings that were used to press records—the gold of the industry. If an artist became popular, masters were often used later for reissued recordings such as greatest hits collections.

No artist, white or black, had ever owned their mas-

Charles signing his ABC contract with Sam Clark in 1959. *(Michael Ochs Archives, Venice, California)*

ters. ABC president Sam Clark explained that to Charles, and the young man behind the dark glasses calmly responded that he understood, but that's what he would like. Afraid of losing the biggest potential pop artist he'd ever signed, Clark gave in on the condition that ABC would own the masters for the first five years. He didn't know that Charles was bluffing and would have accepted ABC's offer even without the masters. The teen-aged rookie, who once would do anything just to get recorded, was now a much wiser music-business veteran.

Charles felt obliged to give his old friends at Atlantic a chance to match the terms but was hardly surprised when they couldn't. Ertegun and Wexler were dismayed by his decision. They had given him complete control of his recordings and had supported him through years of lukewarm sales because they believed in his artistry. Yet no sooner did he break through to the pop charts with a big hit than he dumped Atlantic for another label.

Ertegun and Wexler warned Charles that a label owned by a corporate conglomerate might stress profitability over his creativity. This advice went unheeded. "I didn't want to leave Atlantic," Charles later claimed. "They had treated me wonderfully. And yet, I didn't want to hurt myself. This was a hell of a deal I was being offered." After years of struggling uphill, carrying the two burdens of being blind and being black, Charles was more than willing to put himself first.

The ink was barely dry on his ABC contract when executives there wanted to rush their newest star into the studio for a rousing follow-up to "What'd I Say." But Charles had a different idea. He wanted to record an album of older songs with a "places" theme. And he wanted accompaniment not from his red-hot band but from a string orchestra. Charles had dreamed of playing with a full symphony ever since he listened to classical radio broadcasts as a boy, and this would come very close.

ABC's top brass cringed. They were convinced that teenagers would never buy the old musical chestnuts Ray selected, such as "California, Here I Come," a song first recorded over thirty years before. This was music from their parents' generation, which to them was the worst. "Corny? Hell, yes," Charles acknowledged, "but I'm a corny cat."

Still, ABC handled its new musical investment with care. In 1960, Clark and sales manager Larry Newton agreed to let Ray record the album to get it out of his system so he could get back to the music they wanted. When the twelve tracks were "in the can," however, ABC had to admit that the result sounded beautiful. On a whim, they released the thirty-year-old ballad "Georgia On My Mind" as a single. Then they watched, amazed, as it climbed all the way to number one on *Billboard's* Top 100. It was unclear whether the single's buyers were young, old, or both, but after eleven years of trying, Charles had the most popular record in the nation.

Charles was a hit inside the music business as well. In 1960, "Georgia On My Mind" earned two Grammy Awards, an honor established a few years earlier by a group of industry professionals called the Recording Academy. Charles also took home two more Grammys that year for other performances.

Though Ray's experiment with lush string arrangements succeeded beyond ABC's wildest hopes, he did soon shift back to more familiar R&B turf, as if to show fans that "What'd I Say" was no fluke. Among the new songs he recorded was a rousing give-and-take with the Raeletts called "Hit the Road, Jack," which in 1961 became his next national number one hit.

Then, like a ball in a ping-pong match, Ray bounced as quickly in another direction. He informed ABC that he wanted to cut a country-western album. To Clark and Newton, this was even more bizarre than his previous album concept. Country-western, which had not many years before been known as hillbilly music, was fading in popularity as rock and roll gained strength. Its stronghold was among whites in the segregated South, which added to the absurdity of a black musician selling country songs. There were more strings on a guitar than country stars of color.

Charles's bosses at ABC politely tried to explain this, and he just as courteously ignored them. He was no typical anything and had succeeded against conventional wisdom for years. Besides, Charles considered himself as country as anyone else. He had grown up in the rural South listening to the Grand Ole Opry, had yodeled with the Florida Playboys as a teenager, and even had a final *Billboard* Top 40 hit for Atlantic with

The Grand Ole Opry's historic Ryman Auditorium in Nashville.

a remake of a country song called "I'm Movin' On." There was little Clark and Newton could do but hope for the best.

"I was only interested in two things," Charles pointed out, "being true to myself and being true to the music. I wasn't trying to be

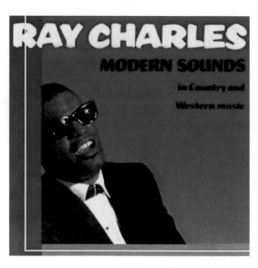

The album cover of Charles's *Modern Sounds in Country and Western Music.*

the first black country singer. I only wanted to take country songs and sing them my way, not the country way." The result, everyone agreed, was not country or R&B, but very distinctly Ray Charles.

Modern Sounds in Country and Western Music was like nothing ever recorded. ABC's fears about alienating listeners proved unnecessary as Southern whites and Northern blacks alike bought it, and it was the number one album nationally for fourteen weeks. A single from the album, "I Can't Stop Loving You," became Charles's third number one pop hit in as many years. Another album cut, "You Don't Know Me," climbed to number two on the pop singles chart.

While country music could trace its roots back before 1925, it certainly received a critical boost in Nashville, Tennessee, that year. The city received two of the most critical items to its future: streetlights and the Grand Ole Opry on Radio WSM. The station itself, Nashville's first, had been on the air only a month when Opry creator George D. Hay blew a train whistle and announced his first guest, an eighty-year-old Texas fiddler named Uncle Jimmy Thompson. After Uncle Jimmy sawed away for an hour, Hay tactfully asked if he hadn't played enough. "Why shucks, a man don't get warmed up in an hour," the white-bearded musician shot back. "I just won an eight-day fiddling contest down in Dallas, Texas, and here's my blue ribbon to prove it."

A flurry of telegrams applauded both the down-home music and the casual atmosphere, and the show was broadcast weekly. By the time Ray Charles heard the Opry as a child, it had become a Saturday night fixture of Southern radio that stretched to four hours, performed before packed houses in Nashville's Ryman Auditorium. Performers emerged from throughout the South, and so did competing live shows, such as the Louisiana Hayride that, in 1948, launched a sensational honky-tonk singer from Alabama named Hank Williams.

Still, Nashville increased its dominance over what became country-western, later shortened to country, music. By the late 1950s, though, the entire musical style was being pounded by the beat of rock and roll. Budding country artists such as Elvis Presley, Jerry Lee Lewis, Buddy Holly, and the Everly Brothers had crossed over to the more lucrative pop charts, and rockabilly musi-

A virtually all-white audience at the Grand Ole Opry. *(Courtesy of Time Life Pictures/ Getty Images.)*

cian Johnny Cash was straddling the fence.

Though Charles recorded *Modern Sounds in Country and Western Music* in New York, it encouraged Nashville recording executives and spawned imitations of his string-heavy arrangements. What became known in the 1960s as the "Nashville Sound" abandoned the twangy fiddles and steel guitars of previous country music for soaring violins behind the voices of new stars such as Patsy Cline and Ray Price.

Though some country artists began to protest against what they felt was a watering down of the music's original unvarnished sound, it wasn't until the 1970s outlaw movement, led by country mavericks such as Willie Nelson, that Nashville abandoned the orchestra pit for good. Later still, Nelson would befriend Charles, and they would team up several times to cover songs across the musical spectrum.

The impact of Charles's journey into country music reached far beyond record sales. It demonstrated that the so-called hillbilly music associated with the South had the same potential for universal appeal as the man who performed it. "Ray Charles did more for country music than any other artist," attests Willie Nelson.

As Charles's fame mushroomed, so did other aspects of his life. His accompanists expanded into the Ray Charles Orchestra, a big band with sixteen instrumentalists and four Raeletts. The road-weary Weenie was retired and replaced at first by a large bus. Then, one day on tour in 1962, the bus full of musicians pulled up to an airport hangar. Ray announced that the forty-four-seat airliner before them was the new band vehicle.

The wide-eyed musicians, still an all-black ensemble, reveled in the plush seats and spotless toilets that never said "Whites Only." They kept flight attendants busy serving up food and drinks, though a sax player from the band remembers there were limits to his boss's splurging: "After a week, Ray being Ray, the stewardesses were gone, and the Raeletts had the job." The truth was that the boss had bought the fast-moving plane largely so he could cram more jobs into a year than the bus would permit.

Charles in the cockpit of his plane. *(Courtesy of Time Life Pictures/Getty Images.)*

Another reason was that he loved the feeling of flight. Charles himself logged much of his time in the cockpit of the plane, peppering the pilot with questions and chatting with airport control towers through a headset. He even flew the plane for short stretches through empty airspace, removing the glass covering the gauge needles so he could feel the rate of climb or descent as he worked the pedals. He claimed he would be able to land the plane if necessary, observing, "That would really be flying blind, baby!"

As the plane moved the band more quickly from gig to gig, it reinforced a determination Charles had already made to stop playing dives such as seedy marathon dances and nightclub stints on the Chitlin Circuit. In 1959, a dance he had played near a military base in North

Carolina had turned ugly. A gunfight erupted that killed one person and wounded others, and Charles sweated bullets of his own as police kept everyone inside until they straightened out the mess.

"I promised myself if I got out alive, I'd never work a dance again," Charles swore. "Being that afraid ain't good for nobody. All you could do was play and pray." Riding high on the success of "What'd I Say," he became a concert-only artist from that point on.

Even as Charles's career was taking off, his private life continued to be in turmoil. He and Della Bea now had three boys, with Robert's birth in 1959. He also had two girls—Evelyn, by his old girlfriend Louise Mitchell, and, in 1960, Raenee, by another girlfriend, Mae Mosely Lyles. Mae had succeeded a woman named Marge Hendricks, who had also borne Ray Charles a son, Charles Wayne. His attitude toward marital fidelity was best described by one of his favorite expressions—"One rooster, many hens"—and he used instances of po-lygamy in the Bible to justify his adultery.

When Ray hit the road with his band, he was on the prowl. As he became a star, more women surrounded him than ever, and he did nothing to discourage them. He also continued using heroin, and the combination of illicit women and drugs signaled trouble to many who knew him privately. They feared that his addiction could careen out of control.

Those present at the recording of "Georgia on My Mind" had been shocked by the sight of one of Ray's girlfriends scratching his bare, bleeding feet, a result of the extreme itchiness that came as a side effect of his heroin abuse. A year later, he almost bled to death from falling into a glass table while high. His six-year-old son saved his life. Ray Jr. went to his father's room to say good night only to find Ray Sr. covered in blood. Della Bea called friends who helped get Charles to the hospital, and they were able to conceal the incident from the press. But Charles had severed a tendon in his arm, which forced him to play concerts one-handed for almost a month.

Despite these private breakdowns, Ray Charles's public face continued to shine. His presence triggered the same excitement at posh A-list venues that it had at roadhouse dances. In 1961, he gave his largest concert to date—"A Salute to Genius"—at the prestigious Hollywood Bowl. Crowded on stage was not only the Ray Charles Orchestra, but a nineteen-piece string section and twelve-voice chorus. Facing them on the other side of a small reflective pool were 6,000 concertgoers, many of them teenagers. Excitement surged throughout the show, and *Downbeat* magazine recorded the crowd response when Ray slammed into his usual finale, "What'd I Say":

> Beyond restraint now, they poured into the aisles . . . in a human torrent down the steps from the cheaper sections to the edge of the pool separating audience from stage. Two youths leaped onto the low wall of

the pool; a dozen followed. In moments the top of the wall was alive. A line of youths was silhouetted against the lighted water, arms madly waving, bodies jerking in ceaseless motion to the music.

Charles's star shined overseas as well. In 1961, he mesmerized Paris during six sold-out concerts. Two years later, the Ray Charles Orchestra embarked on a ten-nation world tour. A spellbound London reporter observed, "A sane train of thought tangles to spaghetti when you try to frame a fragment of that glorious hour and ten minutes when Ray cast a fine mesh net of emotions to ensnare his first British audience."

Though it seemed that Charles had few worlds left to conquer, he found some. He celebrated being the top-

Charles on the balcony of a Paris hotel in 1961. *(Archive Photos)*

The RPM International Building at 2107 West Washington Boulevard in Los Angeles.

selling singles artist of 1962 by forming his own record and music-publishing company. He named it after his favorite fruit, the tangerine. Though he couldn't record directly for Tangerine because of his existing ABC contract, he signed other performers and songwriters, including the one who penned "Hit the Road, Jack." Percy Mayfield had been an up-and-coming musician until he was permanently scarred by a car accident. Now he had success writing hits for others.

Finally, to complete his beginning-to-end ownership of his musical destiny, Charles bought a couple of lots in a nondescript Los Angeles neighborhood in 1963. He transformed the property into RPM International, and it eventually became his recording studio, offices, and such a compelling spiritual base that he sometimes flew home during days off between concerts just to touch the walls he couldn't see. "When you use someone else's property, they call the shots," he noted. "When you own the joint, you rock when you want to rock, roll when you want to roll."

In the early sixties, nobody rocked, rolled, or sang any type of music more convincingly than Ray Charles. The self-assured blind teenager who had so impressed Quincy Jones in Seattle had grown into a man held in almost worshipful esteem by musicians and fans alike. More than ever, the towering talent behind the dark glasses seemed to be his own man.

Under the Rainbow

7

Like his boyhood idol Nat "King" Cole, Ray Charles's cool public exterior hid an inner turmoil that sometimes reached a boiling point. Some of Charles's problems came from American society and popular culture, while others were of his own making.

Though Charles couldn't see, he was far from color blind to the racism he often faced while performing. He once bitterly sounded off, saying, "When you grow up in the southern states of America where anyone colored is treated like dirt, you either grow to accept it or become determined to find something better—even if it kills you."

In the 1950s, the increasing popularity of black R&B artists among young audiences confronted Charles with a new type of segregation. Before, he had often played for predominantly black crowds on the Chitlin Circuit. The few whites at such venues were musical tourists whose presence drew little attention.

By mid-decade, the ascent of rock and roll changed everything. Now young people of both races flocked to Ray's concerts. In segregated areas, many of which were in the South, blacks were separated from whites into rear seating, even though they paid the same ticket price. In 1954, the United States Supreme Court issued a ruling in the landmark case *Brown v. Board of Education* that segregation was unconstitutional, but the process of achieving integration was slow. Since Charles couldn't see audiences, he developed a code with his road manager so he could learn their makeup before he went on stage. If the manager told him "about thirty-seventy, up and down," it meant that the crowd was 30 percent black and 70 percent white, and that blacks were stuck up in the balcony while whites were in front.

Charles had chafed under racism for years because he had no choice, but by 1961 he felt too big to have to endure it any longer. As the civil rights movement raised questions and controversy about racial equality across America, he decided to press the issue at his concerts. Although much of the segregation he faced was at Southern venues, the fuse was actually lit up north when the band played at Yale University in New Haven, Connecticut. Many nonstudents from New Haven's black community purchased tickets, and school officials watched nervously as the show got underway before a mixed crowd they hadn't anticipated. When some black couples switched from sitting to dancing, police moved in and stopped what they claimed was supposed to be a concert for watching only.

Charles was not surprised: "The North was only a hair better than the South. Up there the hatred and prejudice was a bit more subtle, the hypocrisy a little slicker. You could change the lyrics, but the song was still the same everywhere you went."

Within a couple of weeks of the Yale show, Charles was weary enough of racism's refrain to literally stop singing. A student group protested a segregated dance he was to play at a small college in Augusta, Georgia. When informed that only whites would be allowed on the dance floor, Charles refused to play the gig, walking away in front of a cheering student body.

The event's promoter won a lawsuit against Charles for breaking the contract, but he earned wide admiration as one of the first black performers brave enough—and with enough clout—to stand up against racism. By August of that year, another promoter in Memphis, Tennessee, reversed an earlier decision to separate the races, and Charles played that city's first integrated concert of any type for a crowd that, by his code, was about fifty-fifty.

The incident in Georgia made Charles more aware of the impact he could have on the burgeoning civil rights movement. He befriended Martin Luther King Jr., the activist and preacher, and joked with him that he couldn't

By the mid-1960s, the civil rights movement was in full swing across the country. This photograph from the March on Washington for Jobs and Freedom in August 1963 shows civil rights leaders, among them Martin Luther King Jr., A. Philip Randolph, and Roy Wilkins, standing united at the front of the demonstration. *(Library of Congress)*

join him in freedom marches because "[w]hen folks start throwing bricks, I wouldn't know where to run!" Instead, Charles used his influence to help King raise much-needed money. He and the rest of the nation were stunned when, in 1968, King was assassinated in Memphis. Charles joined the thousands of mourners who marched behind King's coffin at his funeral and led the crowd in singing the spiritual "Amen."

In the mid-sixties, the general public learned that Charles could say no to racism but not to drugs. Previous encounters with the law had been brief, and Charles had managed to avoid public exposure as an addict. But the changing times brought increased scrutiny on drug trafficking as the problem expanded outward from a circle made up largely of musicians to a larger group of young adults who were known first as beatniks and later as hippies. Concerned about the spread of drugs, the government cracked down on known or suspected users. Charles's luck finally ran out in 1964 when he was confronted at the airport by federal agents who found heroin and marijuana in his overcoat and more on his plane.

There was no getting off this time. One of the nation's hottest performers faced charges of not just drug possession but smuggling from a foreign country, with a possible prison sentence of up to forty years. Promoters canceled some shows, and getting to the others would

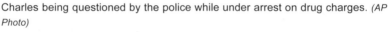

Charles being questioned by the police while under arrest on drug charges. *(AP Photo)*

Ray with Della Bea and their sons, David, Robert, and Ray Jr., at their home in Los Angeles in 1966. *(Courtesy of Time Life Pictures/Getty Images.)*

be much harder since the authorities had impounded the band plane. Charles had to make some very tough decisions.

For the first time in twenty years of performing, he took time off. Charles sat out 1965, vowing to spend time with his wife Della Bea and their three sons at their Los Angeles home. With the prospect of prison hanging over his head, he pondered his next move. The answer came when ten-year-old Ray Jr. cried fiercely when his father had to miss his Little League award presentation because of a recording obligation.

"This kid really loves me," Ray realized. It also dawned on him that if he went to prison, other kids might taunt

Ray Jr., saying, "Your old man's nothing but a jailbird." Charles finally decided, "I ain't ever gonna mess with heroin again."

A doctor offered to help wean Charles off heroin gradually using other less addictive drugs, but he was determined to go "cold turkey"—to stop using drugs all at once and get the withdrawal period over with. He checked into a hospital and waited. After about a day, a tidal wave of nausea flooded every pore of his body.

"I vomited and vomited and vomited till there was nothing left to vomit," he recalled years later. "Then I vomited some more. I was heaving up poison. The poison which was heroin, the poison my body was now naturally rejecting. And it was bitter—bitter as gall. You can't imagine how bitter 'bitter' can be. I was nauseated for hours. My body stunk. My sweat stunk. Everything about me stunk."

As Charles recovered, he learned how to play chess from his doctor and was soon hooked on a healthier habit. "There's no luck in it," he explained, "it's my brain against yours! You've got to outwit, out-think and out-maneuver the other person, and he's thinking how to outwit you."

Chess appealed to Charles's competitive instincts, and he became a ferocious player. He had Braille chessboards made with raised black squares and lowered white ones, and sharpened tops on the black pieces. Opponents had to announce their moves, and Charles would banter back as his fingers flew over the board

Charles playing chess on a board designed especially for him.

feeling the battle: "Uh-huh . . . I see what you're doing, but you ain't gonna do it. I'm gonna move this knight here to king four. Now you stew in your own gravy!"

Charles's proactive approach to kicking his heroin addiction impressed the federal judge hearing his case, and he was granted a one-year, wait-and-see postponement of sentencing to determine whether he could stay clean. He was ordered into a Boston-area hospital for impromptu tests for heroin in his system. There, a musically talented teenager with drug problems of his own wondered if he was hallucinating when he saw his idol in the dining room. The youngster, who later became famous as singer-songwriter James Taylor, would one day sing on Charles's final album.

In the end, Charles kicked heroin for not just a year but the rest of his life. The judge let him off with a $10,000 fine, a slap on the wrist compared to the potential sentence. Although Charles quit heroin, he still smoked marijuana and continued to drink a mixture of coffee and gin. His most obvious drug problems were behind him, but he had not gotten completely sober.

His legal woes weren't over either. Charles sang often about problems with women, and now his life was becoming filled with them. The many different women who had given birth to his children often petitioned him for more support. He paid the women modest amounts of money while his wife unhappily accepted his unfaithfulness as the price of her own affluent life as Mrs. Ray Charles.

In 1964, the year of Charles's drug bust, two of his former girlfriends filed lawsuits demanding more money in child support. In the first case, he argued that he was not the father of the child in question, but lost and was ordered to pay $400 a month. In the second, he "wasn't denying that I was the father. I was just denying that I was the Bank of America." Still, the judge felt that he owed more than he had been paying.

These public airings of Ray's dirty laundry hurt Della deeply. It was one thing to know about his shenanigans, but another to have her face rubbed in it. He could have quietly paid off his accusers. Instead, Charles allowed the cases to become public, humiliating his wife because he couldn't bear to give his former lovers the upper hand. It made Della "nearly sick with anger and grief."

"She's someone who doesn't scream and doesn't yell," Charles observed. "She's not like a kettle which will explode without a valve. She's more like a pot which is half-filled with coffee and left on the stove all night. Finally, the coffee will just burn itself out. So for years, she just burned."

Finally, in 1976, Della Bea had had enough. She filed for divorce. Ray continued his amorous extracurricular adventures, eventually fathering at least twelve children, mostly by unmarried women who were then left to raise those children alone.

Charles's now-tarnished public image was countered with news about his charitable activities. In addition to his support for the civil rights movement in America, he became an outspoken critic of South African apartheid. Even as American blacks were fighting for integration, millions of South Africans were being forcibly moved from their homes to new locations in order to uphold the government's policy of strict segregation of all races. Though apartheid would stay in place until the early 1990s, Charles was among those who helped draw attention to the racism abroad as well as at home.

Charles meeting with President Richard Nixon at the White House in 1972. *(National Archives)*

Charles began meeting with U.S. chiefs of state in 1972, when he visited the White House to convince then-President Richard Nixon of the need for sickle-cell anemia research. Sickle-cell anemia has no cure and affects mainly people of West African descent. Charles reported that meeting Nixon was a "gas," but upheld his policy of not signing autographs, which were difficult because of his blindness. In turning down a request from the president, Charles reasoned that the "surest way to get folks pissed at you is to do something for Mary that you wouldn't do for Jane."

Another cause Charles was proud to support was the state of Israel. During the civil rights movement, many black workers were helped and encouraged by members of the Jewish faith. In turn, many African Americans supported the Jewish people in their efforts to establish a Jewish state in the Middle East. Charles played concert tours in Israel, explaining that his sympathy for the Jewish plight came from a shared history of persecution. Awards and recognition from the Jewish community moved him deeply, and he was always proud of having met with David Ben-Gurion, a former prime minister of Israel.

In the end, what hit Charles hardest in the sixties was not sex and drugs but rock and roll. He had slipped from his position as the top-selling pop artist in 1962 to a still-respectable number four in 1963, and he now had seven Grammys inscribed with his name. Then came the Beatles. The group, which credited Charles as one of its greatest inspirations, led a British invasion that toppled him and other American veterans such as Elvis Presley from the charts. Eventually, stateside artists responded to Beatlemania with emerging styles of their own, such as black-produced music categorized as soul and the psychedelic sound of West Coast bands.

SOUL MAN

Charles's rhythmic blend of R&B, gospel, and piano-driven jazz defied categorization. It wasn't quite rock and roll, but what was it?

In coming years, other black artists would also become popular but hard to define. At a Detroit Ray Charles show in 1961, Steveland Morris, a ten-year-old local harmonica and piano prodigy who idolized Charles, was permitted to join him on stage for a couple of numbers. Until then the boy hadn't realized that, like himself, his musical hero was blind. In another two years the boy recorded an album called "A Tribute to Uncle Ray" under the stage name of Stevie

Wonder and went on to become one of the most successful artists of his generation.

Another Detroit teenager sang gospel music in her father's church in the 1950s but secretly longed to wail like lead Raelett Margie Hendricks in a hot band like Ray's. The girl, Aretha Franklin, endured years of being overlooked before signing with Charles's former producer, Atlantic's Jerry Wexler. The result was a number one hit, "Respect," and a career that amassed more million-selling songs than any other woman in recording history. In 1968, Franklin realized her dream, acting as a Raelett in a vocal duet with Charles for a popular Coca-Cola commercial, recorded in his own RPM Studio.

Young Stevie Wonder and Marvin Gaye recording together at Motown Records in Detroit.

Wonder and many other breakthrough black artists of the 1960s recorded for a new independent Detroit label called Motown, launched in the home of Berry Gordy, an African-American entrepreneur only a year older than Charles. Gordy promoted his stable of successful artists as "Hitsville U.S.A.," and the sound collectively became known as soul. Charles was considered the music's spiritual father, though his record sales began to slip just as new soul artists were catching on.

> "Everyone at Motown idolized Ray," confirmed Marvin Gaye, one of the most respected soul artists. "He had both the commercial success and raw feeling we were looking for. He was the man."
>
> Charles himself was constantly asked over the years to define soul, a type of music he is usually credited with pioneering. Sometimes his answer was offhanded, as when he called it "just the way black folks sing when they leave themselves alone." One of his most thoughtful reflections came in 1966 when the label was still new: "Soul is when you take a song and make it part of you—a part that's so true, so real, people think that it must have happened to you . . . it's like electricity; we don't really know what it is, do we? But it's a force that can light a room."

The newly popular artists on both sides of the Atlantic were usually younger than Charles, who wasn't yet forty. In the space of a few years, he had been washed from pop music's mainstream. The full-blown Ray Charles Orchestra sounded dated in an era of guitar-driven bands whose members could usually fit into a sedan. The violins on his album arrangements were tame compared to those on the searing Stratocaster guitar of Jimi Hendrix, a onetime sideman for Little Richard who was now taking rock in a new direction.

Charles fought back by trying to tap into newer territory. He recorded soulful versions of recent hits such as the Beatles' "Yesterday" and "Eleanor Rigby," but they charted far lower than the originals. In 1972, he recorded *Message to the People,* an ambitious theme album showcasing what he felt was good and bad about his country.

Charles had high hopes for that album, which was highlighted by a stirring rendition of "America the Beautiful," arranged by his old friend Quincy Jones. Jones was a jazz musician but found greater success behind the scenes as a composer and producer for projects ranging from albums to film soundtracks. Charles was disappointed that his new project peaked at number fifty-two, while the politically charged album *What's Going On?*—released around the same time by one of his disciples, the soul singer Marvin Gaye—hit number six and spawned three top ten singles.

Charles tried to be philosophical. "Sometimes I've clipped the nasty reviews I've gotten," he explained, "and hung 'em on the wall. Just put 'em there to show myself they ain't gonna kill me. My music's not about pleasing critics. It's about pleasing me."

But his record label of fourteen years, ABC, was less patient. Executives suggested that Charles apply his gospel-infused style to an album of genuinely sacred songs, but he replied, "My mother said you can't serve two masters, and I sing rhythm and blues." ABC now regarded him as a has-been talent who could no longer reach out to a new generation of record buyers. The artist who once gave the label a record that sold three million copies was dropped in 1974.

Trying to spark the lightning of his earlier career, Charles returned to Atlantic where Ahmet Ertegun and Jerry Wexler were still at the helm. Though they had been hurt deeply when Charles left them for ABC, Ertegun

Charles with Wexler and Ertegun after his return to Atlantic in the 1970s. *(Globe Photo)*

and Wexler had persevered and eventually found tremendous success of their own. Though they knew Charles was as hardheaded and self-centered as ever, they were persuaded to welcome him back to the Atlantic fold. Still, after an album of beautiful but dated music flopped, Charles stumbled even harder on subsequent efforts trying to emulate the disco sound that was currently popular but ill-suited to his talents.

Charles had better luck on the road, where longtime fans attended concerts largely to hear his old hits. Even so, by the end of the 1970s these crowds were thinning as well. At one low point, only seventy people showed up for a show in Memphis. Few of Ray's R&B contemporaries were faring better. Chuck Berry was in jail for tax evasion, and Little Richard had given up music to become a minister.

Despite making monthly payments to the mothers of his many children, Charles was still a wealthy man who could afford to bow out gracefully as a recording and performing artist. He could generate some extra income by renting his cutting-edge studio to others, and perhaps even produce their records. There was only one catch: he couldn't stand on the sidelines and still be Ray Charles. He had been in perpetual motion since childhood and welcomed the notion of retirement as much as that of death. Right or wrong, he had to keep moving.

He's the Right One, Baby!

8

As the 1970s began, Ray Charles was no longer at the forefront of popular music. Not that the music industry had forgotten him. Leading record producers and performers of all types respected his talents and acknowledged his influence on their styles. They affectionately called him Brother Ray, which became the title of his autobiography, published in 1978. He even received a Grammy Award for a blistering rendition of a Stevie Wonder hit, "Living for the City," even though the album that spawned it only reached a disappointing 178 on the *Billboard* charts. Charles had received this highest honor from music professionals nine times before, but always for his hit singles and albums from the sixties. He appreciated this ongoing recognition from his peers, but wished others felt likewise during this dip in his popularity.

Slowly, the general public did begin to rediscover Ray. In 1979, the Georgia State Legislature proclaimed Ray's version of "Georgia on My Mind" the official state song, and invited him to the capital of his birth state to dedicate it in a live performance. His stirring rendition left a packed gallery of politicians misty-eyed and cheering.

Charles planted the seeds for a nationwide comeback with an appearance on *Saturday Night Live*, which at the time was a new, edgy comedy show hugely popular with young adults. As the show's guest host, he not only sang

Charles, at the height of his comeback, is photographed here with two of his sons: David *(left)* and Ray Jr. *(Globe Photo)*

but also appeared in skits. In one, a record producer rejected his version of "What'd I Say" in favor of a cut by a bubbly white group called the Young Caucasians. This direct parody of rock and roll's early days in the 1950s, when white musicians cut sterile versions of black R&B music, drew laughs and new attention and respect for Charles as the real deal.

Saturday Night Live stars John Belushi and Dan Ackroyd liked Charles so much that they featured him and other soul singers, including Aretha Franklin and James Brown, in their 1980 comedy film *The Blues Brothers.* Charles was funny as the blind owner of a music store who casually shot a would-be shoplifter hoping for an easy theft, and red-hot when he broke into "Shake a Tail Feather." Such appearances proved that Charles continued to be cool even at age fifty, and they cemented his reputation as one of the fathers of modern popular music.

Along with seeing Charles's face on television and at the movies, people began to once again hear his voice as oldies stations sprung up across the radio dial. Their playlists were devoted to pop hits from the 1950s and '60s, giving "What'd I Say" its greatest airplay since it was first released. Still, Charles didn't want to be shelved as an oldies artist. The question was, since Charles had blazed so many musical trails, which way should he turn?

He got an idea for a new direction when he recorded a novelty number called "Beers to You" with actor Clint

Eastwood for his movie *Any Which Way You Can*. Neither the song nor the film was very memorable, but "Beers" crept onto the country music charts, reaching number fifty. Recalling his all-time top seller from twenty years before, "I Can't Stop Loving You," Charles decided that perhaps it was time for another journey down the country road.

Charles recorded a country music album in 1983, this time without the string orchestra and multi-voiced chorus that had backed his breakthrough effort a generation ago. His newest arrangements were stripped down to Charles accompanied by a small group of Nashville sidemen. The album sold modestly, but produced a song that rose to number twenty on the country charts. Once that might have been a lackluster result. Now, it was Charles's biggest hit in fifteen years.

After a follow-up album generated lukewarm response, Charles decided to try a collection of duets with some of his favorite country singers, including Willie Nelson, George Jones, and Johnny Cash. The result was an album called *Friendship*, which included five country hits. Among them was "Seven Spanish Angels" with Nelson, which became a number one country song in 1985. Ray Charles was back.

As he had with his musical business ventures such as RPM, Charles began diversifying his methods of performing. He would play shows with his big band and the Raeletts, but also played concerts with established city orchestras using only a few of his key musicians. These

Charles with Nancy and Ronald Reagan after singing "America the Beautiful" at the Republican National Convention in 1984. *(Corbis)*

"string gigs" allowed him for the first time to play some of his full-blown album cuts with orchestral accompaniment, just as they were recorded.

One of the most popular songs emerging from Charles's string gigs was his version of "America the Beautiful," which he had recorded to little fanfare back in 1972. In 1984, both the Democratic and Republican parties tried to coax Charles to their presidential conventions to sing it. The Democrats wanted a free performance while the Republicans offered a hefty fee, so Charles sang "America the Beautiful" beside President Ronald Reagan amidst a sea of flags as millions of television viewers looked on.

The scene was repeated six months later at the inaugural ball after Reagan was reelected. Dozens of celebrities had already performed before it was time for the grand finale. Frank Sinatra, himself a singing legend, introduced Ray Charles, then led him to his piano amid thunderous applause to once again sing "America the Beautiful." The Charles-inspired version soon became such a favorite rendition of the patriotic song that many felt it should replace "The Star-Spangled Banner" as the American national anthem.

Charles brushed off criticism from civil rights activists, who accused him of glorifying America in song while disregarding racial injustices that still existed in the U.S. Reagan, who had initially opposed the Civil Rights Act and Voting Rights Act in the 1960s and frequently chastised people on welfare, was not a favorite of many African-American leaders. "I'm the first to say this country is racist to the bone," Charles countered, "but that doesn't mean I can't be patriotic. For all the b.s. about America, I still work and live here in comfort."

Within a few years, Charles had fought back from near-obscurity to the A-list of most-desired performers for any big event. In 1985, he was one of more than forty of the biggest stars in the music business to join forces and record "We Are the World," with proceeds going to famine relief in Africa. The gathering of musicians, which included Michael Jackson, Stevie Wonder, Bob Dylan, Bruce Springsteen, Willie Nelson, Paul Simon, and Tina Turner, fell silent as the familiar dark glasses entered the room.

"That's like the Statue of Liberty walking in," marveled Billy Joel, who, despite having already charted two number one hits of his own, trembled as he was introduced to Charles. The object of all the attention sat down at his piano bench and reflected on his own visits to impoverished areas of Africa during concert tours: "I've put my hands on these children, and their skin feels like cellophane on bone. That's unreal stuff."

With Charles's longtime cohort Quincy Jones at the helm as producer, each superstar was squeezed into a cameo appearance on the song. Charles's famous ad-libs soared over the final chorus. "We Are the World" topped the pop charts for four weeks and raised hundreds of thousands of dollars for famine relief.

Through the 1980s, Charles's star continued to glitter across the globe, sometimes in astonishing places. In 1989,

Charles is photographed here at a Hollywood dinner party in the mid-1980s with his old friend from his days in Seattle, Quincy Jones. *(Globe Photo)*

he scored a number one single in Japan with "Ellie My Love," and topped European pop charts with the song "Till the Next Somewhere." Though his new recordings weren't selling as briskly back home, he won his eleventh Grammy in 1990 for "I'll Be Good to You," a dance-friendly duet with fellow soul veteran Chaka Khan.

With the 1990s came a career turn that even the calculating Charles hadn't foreseen. He was tapped by Diet Pepsi to do television commercials. It wasn't the first time he was sought as a pitchman. Since his Coke ads of the sixties, Ray had appeared most famously in 1988 as a California Raisin, lending his voice to an animated fruit wearing sunglasses.

His "You've Got the Right One, Baby" Diet Pepsi campaign put him squarely back on the national stage,

Charles appears at the piano, surrounded by the "Uh Huh!" girls, in one of the famous Diet Pepsi advertisements that revitalized his popularity.

treating his blindness with gentle humor. After sipping from a Diet Coke can next to his piano, Charles asked, "Who's the wise guy?" before getting his Diet Pepsi back and smiling, "Now *that's* the right one, baby!"

Even more successful were a new series of "Uh-Huh!" ads launched during football's Super Bowl in 1991. First, a series of candidates from a punk rocker to a dog attempt Charles's trademark line. Then the man himself, flanked by "Uh-Huh!" girls suggesting the Raeletts, shows in rollicking song that he—and the Diet Pepsi on his piano—are truly the right ones.

The public agreed, and the spots were judged America's most popular commercials of 1991. Charles was so familiar to young viewers that in airports, children often recognized him before their parents did. The reborn musical saint was becoming not just the father but the grandfather of soul.

As if to answer critics who accused Charles of selling out to shill products on TV, he went back to the studio to record another album. It yielded "A Song for You" and another Grammy in 1993. He was now one of the few

LADIES AND GENTLEMEN . . . THE GRAMMYS

Ray Charles was not the only big musical influence to emerge from Los Angeles in the 1950s. In 1957, two years before Charles stormed the pop charts, a group of industry participants banded together to form the Recording Academy to share their experiences and celebrate their achievements. Their goal was to recognize artists not by how many records they sold but by the quality of their music. They also

The Grammy Award trophy.

wanted to showcase the achievements of behind-the-scenes contributors such as songwriters, recording engineers, and producers.

The next year, their efforts led to the first of the now-famous Grammy Awards for recording achievements. The twenty-eight winners from the first year of the Grammys reflected little of the rock-and-roll craze that had taken hold. Pop recording awards were dominated by the likes of jazz masters Count Basie and Ella Fitzgerald, and the only R&B award for that year went to a white group, the Champs, for their number one hit "Tequila."

As the Recording Academy spread to other cities and gained thousands of new members, the size and stature of the Grammy Awards also increased. By 1960, when Charles earned four Grammys for two songs and an album, thirty-nine total awards were given. Today over one hundred Grammys are awarded each year in categories ranging from R&B to rock, gospel to rap.

True to the goals of the Grammy founders, the most popular artists have not always hauled home the trophies. The Beatles, who have had the most number one pop hits during the Grammy era, only won seven awards as a band. Elvis Presley, next in chart success, only received three. However, early definitions of good music were so narrow that the award was sometimes labeled the "Granny" by young rock and rollers who were shut out until the Beatles broke through in 1966.

Charles's twenty Grammys came over a span of forty-five years. He has also received a Lifetime Achievement Award, and his songs "What'd I Say" and "I Can't Stop Loving You" are in the Grammy Hall of Fame. Charles is not the biggest winner, though. That distinction goes to orchestra conductor Georg Solti, who has received thirty-eight Grammys. In second place, with twenty-seven awards for performing, composing, and arranging, is Charles's old buddy Quincy Jones.

artists to earn the coveted award at least once in three different decades, with more awards to come in yet another decade.

Even a couple of physical scares during his comeback years couldn't ground him. In 1985, Charles's band plane, by now a turboprop jet, overshot the runway at a small airport and crash-landed in a muddy Indiana cornfield. Charles was hurled to the floor, but he and the other passengers escaped serious injury. Still, the experience was scary and he flew commercial airlines for the rest of his days.

Charles was even more frightened when he began hearing a constant echo of "sounds within sounds," a nightmare for the musical ear of an artist who had joked that he "could hear a rat pee on cotton." Being blind hadn't stopped him, but going deaf could kill his career.

The problem turned out to be correctable, but the scare shook up Charles so much that in 1987, he traveled to Washington, D.C., to urge Congress to increase funding for hearing-loss research. "Most people take their

THE BLIND LEADING THE DEAF

As bad as blindness was, the prospect of being deaf terrified Ray. "I'm too old to be Helen Keller," he said. After testifying before the U.S. Senate about the importance of increased federal money for hearing-loss research, he told his ear specialist, Jack Pulec, that he wanted to fight deafness with his wallet as well as his words. Pulec came up with some ideas and the Ray Charles Foundation, endowed with $1 million, was off and running.

The initial focus of the foundation was to improve the development of cochlear implants, a technology to help profoundly deaf people. Unlike conventional hearing aids, which amplify existing sounds, cochlear devices electronically stimulate the auditory nerve to help pick up sound waves. They are surgically implanted in patients' ear canals, unlike removable hearing aids. Thanks to help from the Ray Charles Foundation, thousands of underprivileged children have received cochlear implants.

"It's amazing to watch these kids who have never heard anything in their life get these implants, and a year or so later they can hear and talk," Charles reflected. "It gives you a great feeling; I love that."

Charles gave millions of dollars to the foundation. As time went on, the charitable efforts came to reflect the diversity of his interests. In the last two decades of his life, he donated millions to small, predominantly black colleges. The Ray Charles Foundation formalized a quiet activism displayed ever since Charles gained the personal and financial clout to make a difference.

hearing for granted," he explained. "I can't. My eyes are my handicap, but my ears are my opportunity. My ears show me what my eyes can't."

As he approached his fiftieth anniversary in show business at age sixty-five, Ray Charles's status as a legend was sealed. He could retire at the height of his career. Except for his yearlong hiatus in 1965, however, Charles had never even taken a real vacation. "I don't understand what retirement is," he maintained, "and I don't intend to find out."

Final Verse

9

By the mid-1990s, Charles himself rivaled "America the Beautiful" as a national institution. Worshipful tributes filled the airwaves: a public television documentary; a star-studded salute to his fiftieth anniversary in show business; and a guest slot on the children's series *Sesame Street.* The sexagenarian still wasn't generating chart toppers, but his five-decade musical catalog was repackaged in new collections, one filled with five CDs.

On the road, Charles barnstormed harder than ever, hopscotching the world for more than two hundred days a year to play events of all types. The show was by now a well-oiled musical machine, one he could easily control. Like many blind people, Charles thrived on the familiarity of set routines. "Been saying this for forty years," he admitted, "and I'm still saying it: Sweetheart,

Charles at the piano during a celebration commemorating his fiftieth year in show business. *(AP Photo)*

I don't change."

When Charles repeated a visit to a city, he tried to stay at the same suite at the same hotel whenever he could. In the room, he first checked and memorized all the exits. Then he took small steps to important locations in the room, whistling a tune in rhythm to his stride to measure the distances. Using his musical method, the bathroom might be four bars from his bed and the refrigerator six. In the kitchen a fresh supply of milk, fruit, and hot coffee always awaited him. Charles's road manager was required to book a suite a full day ahead of his stay to make sure everything would be perfect.

Occasionally, Charles literally ran into rooms outside the norm. Once, he checked into a glamorous Las Vegas hotel suite with a bed that was perched two steps above the floor. "You know, I think these people are trying to kill me," he joked.

Charles's traveling wardrobe contained several different performing tuxedos, and he usually chose his own outfit before a show. From his brief sighted childhood he could recall colors such as red, blue, black, and white, though more recent designer hues such as teal were foreign to him. He distinguished his tuxes by touch, learning differences in fabric and the location of buttons or pockets. He could tell brown from black shoes by special markings he scratched into their soles.

Outside Charles's cocoon, his band was accompanied by a virtual clothing store. Musicians wore matching outfits, and on extended tours took up to eight changes each. This meant that road managers might need to stay on top of about one hundred shirts, jackets, and trousers, not to mention a few dozen sequined gowns for the Raeletts.

If moving the Ray Charles Orchestra across the globe required intense organization and discipline, playing for Charles could be even more challenging. Charles often smiled that he was easy to work with as long as you were perfect, and he was only half kidding. The visual uncertainties caused by blindness conditioned him to seek routines and control all aspects of his life wherever he could. He wore a Braille watch and had his shows planned to the second.

Charles's manager of more than forty years, Joe Adams, used an authoritarian but efficient system of rules and fines to ensure that all band members were on time. Infractions included arriving at the bandstand less than thirty minutes early to wearing the wrong-colored socks. Adams compiled a long list, most of which carried at least a fifty-dollar fine. The charges were usually pooled into a fund for a year-end band party, but frequent offenders rarely enjoyed it because of a final rule Charles adapted from baseball: three strikes and you're out.

Many musicians, unaccustomed to the structured lifestyle, had to change their habits to appear with Ray. What surprised some was how much they had to sharpen their playing skills as well. They learned that their sightless boss had an uncanny ability to distinctly hear each instrument in a seventeen-piece band.

"He'd know it if the bass missed a note, a single note," reported a member of Charles's entourage. "He'd know it if the drummer's left shoelace was flapping. You be with us long enough, you'll swear the man can see." Band members carried charts for over five dozen songs that Charles might possibly play. He picked about a third of them shortly before he went on, and the band received his selections in code numbers—nobody called the songs by name—about five minutes before show time.

Compounding the just-in-time announcement of each night's set list was the fact that Charles never played a song the same way twice. Musicians learned to watch his legs and feet, which stomped and thrashed to his desired tempo. "You know you're getting a good show when Ray's socks fall down," explained one of his associates. "His feet are going up over the piano. One sock falls half-mast. It's because of all the energy he expends."

These piano dances, which were accompanied by his upper body swaying so much it barely clung to its perch on the bench, were as endearing to audiences as Charles's singing and playing. It was what they expected to see. And despite changes in the set list, there were many other constants in an evening with Ray Charles. The orchestra warmed up with a couple of numbers before Ray, introduced as "The Genius of Soul," was escorted to his piano bench while making a sweeping gesture that pretended to pull the entire audience into his joyful embrace.

Charles usually started with a few quieter numbers, such as "Georgia on My Mind," before shifting to Raelett time. "I just want to bring forth a little femininity, you know, to sort of perk up my spirits," he might say. "You know how it is when you got an old battery like mine; you got to keep it charged up." The Raeletts swayed onto the stage and joined Charles off and on through numbers that usually included "America the Beautiful" and always climaxed with "What'd I Say." Wanting to leave the audience buzzing on that high note, he hardly ever performed encores.

In contrast to his original band, the Ray Charles Orchestra of the 1990s was a revolving door of young musicians often eager to put some name-band experience on their resume and then move on. Unlike his earliest musicians, the newcomers were as likely to be white as black. Comedian Bill Cosby once noted to Charles at a jazz festival, "Your band is all white."

"That's funny," Charles responded, "they don't *sound* white."

By now, Charles knew very little about his musicians

Ray Charles is photographed mid-laugh while appearing on television with his friend, the comedian Bill Cosby. *(Courtesy of Getty Images.)*

except how well they followed their charts on stage. Blindness had always made him feel somewhat isolated from others and triggered behaviors such as eating alone because he didn't want to appear awkward in public. Age and fame deepened his separation from others, and he was sometimes seen as antisocial.

"There are ups and downs in working for him," reported David Hoffman, a trumpeter during the band's later years. "He can be decidedly unpleasant at times, and extremely self-centered. I think he has forgotten the people that ensured his success, like many people in his position."

On the other hand, musicians such as Hoffman relished the experience of learning from one of the most respected pros in the business. "On those best nights, the ebb and flow of the time made the twenty-two musicians in the band seem like an extension of Ray's limbs and body," he recalled. "He would turn to the band with a 'yeah' that indicated that he was happy with the music. I think he lived for those moments. To that end he employed a band of twenty-two musicians when most other artists had scaled back or used 'pick-up' bands in order to save money. But to Ray nothing was comparable to the sound of his hand-picked band. We understood what he was after, we could read his movements, we had the insight of working with him night after night, realizing what he wanted and being able to accomplish it."

Concerts progressed so seamlessly that they were sometimes accused of being too commercial, especially when compared to the raucous Chitlin Circuit shows that paved Charles's climb to the top. "I thought I had *always* been commercial," he shot back. "I had always been in the business of making money."

Though some felt that Charles's concerts were becoming a bit predictable, most agreed that, especially for his age, he was still a heck of a performer. As his number of career shows approached 10,000, there were few important venues in the world where music's most soulful senior citizen hadn't played. Sometimes he was still a pioneer, as in 2002, when he made history by headlining the first music concert in the 2,000-year-old Roman Colosseum.

As age finally slowed his pursuit of women, Charles spent most of his non-performing time at his "Soul Bunker," as insiders called his RPM studio in Los Angeles. Here, in another environment designed especially for him, he felt comfortable and in control. When the lights brought in for a photography session blew a circuit in the building, Charles leaped from the piano stool where he had been posing.

"Circuit breakers?" he shouted. "*I'm* the one who knows that, babe. Lemme see what you're talking about!" Charles's valet escorted him to a utility closet. As the astonished photo crew watched, the blind man fingered the switches until he found the one that had tripped off.

Even when Charles passed age seventy in the new millennium, it seemed to his fans that he could go on forever. "I've known times when I've felt terrible," he admitted, "but once I get on stage and the band starts with the music . . . it's like you have pain and take an aspirin, and you don't feel it no more." That's why it came as a surprise to many when, in August 2003, Charles cancelled an entire tour for the first time in fifty-three years on the road.

The official reason given was an orthopedic problem that was corrected by hip replacement surgery. Those close to Charles, however, knew that his decades of hard living, still fueled by the coffee-and-gin concoction he downed daily, were finally catching up to him. Though his hip could be fixed, Charles's liver was failing rapidly. The Ray Charles Orchestra was grounded for good.

Even though Charles was obviously ill, he impressed people as always with his keen awareness of what he couldn't see. Astride a bicycle in a photo shoot for *Esquire* magazine, he complained, "This is a girl's bike, man! Why would I be riding a girl's bike? You didn't think I was gonna notice that, right? You guys are trying to sucker a blind man!"

At one of his last performances, a televised VIP banquet attended by U.S. president George W. Bush, Charles struggled through "Georgia on My Mind" and "America the Beautiful." In April 2004, he could barely speak at the celebrity-studded dedication of his RPM studios as a historic landmark.

The timing of RPM's enshrinement was appropriate because for the past nine months Charles had focused his remaining strength there for one final project. He

Charles, age seventy, on the keyboard during a concert in 2000. *(AP Photo)*

wanted to record an album of duets with some of his
favorite performers—from established artists of his
vintage, such as Willie Nelson and fellow Chitlin Circuit
graduate B. B. King, to more recent stars like pop/jazz
diva Norah Jones. As in his earliest recording years, he
wanted to give the project a live feeling by recording
with all the singers and backup musicians in one room
in as few takes as possible. Besides the desired sponta-
neity, there was also the practical consideration that
Charles didn't have the energy for many retakes.

The first recording actually was live, captured when
singer Van Morrison was inducted by his idol into the
Songwriters Hall of Fame. After the ceremony they
treated the crowd to a rousing version of the Morrison
song "Crazy Love," and its author hailed Ray as "a soul
brother in every sense of the word."

Mutual admiration continued as, one by one, some of

the biggest names in the business were invited to come in and lay down a track with Charles. King was first, and the two old R&B masters exchanged sizzling piano and guitar licks on "Sinner's Prayer," which Charles had initially recorded fifty years earlier. They laughingly agreed that had they known they'd be around this long, they would have taken better care of themselves. James Taylor, in his first brush with his fellow former heroin addict since their hospital encounter, proclaimed that of his five favorite all-time artists, the top three were Charles. Blues stylist Bonnie Raitt reported that upon meeting him for the first time, "Rockets went off. I could have sung, 'Row, row, row your boat' with him and been thrilled."

The sessions weren't all smiles. Charles had a bed in the studio to rest when necessary, and at times he was clearly struggling. Nelson laid his hand on Ray's shoulder and encouraged him through their poignant reading of the reflective lyrics in the old Frank Sinatra hit "It Was a Very Good Year." When Charles finished his final album track with Elton John of the pop star's song "Sorry Seems to Be the Hardest Word," everyone in the studio was wet-eyed. They feared that after more than fifty years and sixty albums, Charles might be recording for the last time.

Three months later, on June 10, 2004, Ray Charles died of liver disease at age seventy-three. Though the U.S. was officially mourning the death of former president Ronald Reagan just five days earlier, many felt that the flags at half-mast through-out the nation rec-ognized the genius of soul as much as the commander in chief. The *New Yorker* magazine reflected popular sentiment with a cover mockup of a ten-dollar bill domi-nated by Charles's face.

The *New Yorker* cover from the week of Charles's death.

Charles's body lay for a day of public visitation at the Los Angeles Convention Center, a few feet from a black grand piano containing scores of "Georgia on My Mind" and "What'd I Say." On the empty piano bench was one of Charles's vivid tuxedo jackets, and on his face in the open coffin were his trademark dark glasses. More than 5,000 fans filed past to bid him farewell.

At a private funeral service the following day, his old friends Nelson, King, Stevie Wonder, and others deliv-ered often tearful musical tributes before trumpeter Wynton Marsalis played the spiritual "Down By the Riverside" as a final farewell.

Charles's final album, *Genius Loves Company,* was

Legendary guitarist B. B. King in an emotional moment during his performance at Ray Charles's funeral on June 19, 2004. *(AP Photo)*

released about two months later. In a week, it soared to number two on *Billboard's* Top 100 album chart, eventually hit the top spot after the Grammys, and became Charles's best seller of all time, achieving multi-platinum status.

Not long after the album's release, the movie *Ray* opened in theaters to critical praise. This tuneful, honest biopic featured an Oscar-nominated performance by Jamie Foxx. The movie was also nominated for Best Picture and four other awards in the annual recognition of film excellence.

The crowning achievement to Charles's career occurred in February 2005 when the singer achieved a posthumous near-sweep of the Grammys with *Genius Loves Company*, which took home eight of the ten awards for which it was nominated. Included among the accumulated trophies were album of the year and record of the year for the song "Here We Go Again," his duet with Norah Jones. He also proved his versatility once again by winning gospel and pop categories. The awards, while a recognition of the quality of Charles's final recordings, were also a testament to the durability of his career, his ability to work in numerous genres, and the far-reaching excellence of Ray Charles's music.

Timeline

1930   Ray Charles Robinson is born September 30 in Albany, Georgia.

1935   Brother George drowns.

1937   After losing his sight, Charles is sent to the Florida School for the Deaf and the Blind.

1945   Quits school and for the next two years works as a musician in Jacksonville, Orlando, and Tampa.

1948   Moves to Seattle and forms the McSon Trio.

1949   Records "Confession Blues" on Down Beat Records, which reaches number five on the R&B charts.

1950   Moves to L.A. and begins touring on the Chitlin Circuit.

1951   Marries and divorces within a year.

1952   Begins recording on Atlantic Records.

1954   Gets own touring band.

1955   "I Got a Woman" becomes number two R&B hit; marries second wife, Della Beatrice Howard.

1956   "Drown in My Own Tears" becomes his first number one R&B song; records first album, *The Great Ray Charles.*

1959   "What'd I Say" reaches number six on the pop charts; switches labels to ABC Records.

1960   "Georgia on My Mind" becomes his first number one pop hit.

1961 "Hit the Road, Jack" reaches number one on the pop charts; makes first European tour; refuses to play segregated college dance in Augusta; successfully plays first integrated concert in Memphis history.

1962 *Modern Sounds in Country and Western Music* becomes his first number one pop album; includes hit singles "I Can't Stop Loving You" (number one) and "You Don't Know Me" (number two); Charles forms own music publishing company.

1963 Builds RPM International complex with recording studio and offices.

1964 Convicted of heroin possession, kicks his habit.

1974 Is dropped by ABC after years of slow record sales.

1975 Receives tenth Grammy Award for "Living for the City."

1976 Is divorced by Della Bea.

1979 Georgia Legislature names his recording of "Georgia on My Mind" the official state song; his appearance on the TV show *Saturday Night Live* begins his comeback in popularity.

1980 Appears in the popular movie *The Blues Brothers.*

1984 Sings "America the Beautiful" at the Republican National Convention and the Reagan inauguration.

1985 Scores number one country hit with "Seven Spanish Angels"; featured on "We Are the World" charity recording of musical superstars.

1989 Wins Grammy for "I'll Be Good to You"; despite modest U.S. record sales, has number one hits in Europe and Japan.

1991 "You've Got the Right One, Baby!" Diet Pepsi commercials are rated most popular advertisements of the year.

1993 Wins Grammy for "A Song for You."

2002 Headlines first concert in 2,000-year history of Roman Colosseum.

2003   Cancels first entire tour in fifty-three years due to failing health; performs for last time later that year.

2004   Makes last public appearance as his RPM Studio is declared a historic site; dies June 10 in Los Angeles; *Genius Loves Company*, made during the final months of his life, is released posthumously. It reaches number one on *Billboard's* Top 100 album chart and becomes his best-selling recording ever; biographical movie *Ray* is released four months after his death.

2005   *Genius Loves Company* brings home eight Grammys. *Ray* is nominated for six Oscars, including best picture and best actor for Jamie Foxx.

Sources

CHAPTER ONE: Roots in Florida Clay

p. 12, "Even compared to other blacks . . ." Ray Charles, "Ray Charles Biography," RayCharles.com: The Official Site, http://www.raycharles.com.

p. 14, "You don't hit . . ." "Ray Charles Interview," National Visionary Leadership Project, http://www.visionaryproject.com/NVLPmemberTier/visionariesT1/VisionaryPages/CharlesRay/transcript.pdfinterview, 2002: 11 (accessed January 13, 2005)

p. 14, "Come over here, boy," Ray Charles and David Ritz, *Brother Ray* (New York: Da Capo Press, 1992), 9.

CHAPTER TWO: Into the Darkness

p. 21, "I'm afraid the boy's . . ." Charles and Ritz, *Brother Ray*, 16.

p. 22, "He's blind, but . . ." National Visionary Leadership Interview, 9.

p. 24, "I honestly had never heard . . ." Thomas Thompson, "Music Soaring in a Darkened World," *Life*, July 19, 1966, 61.

p. 25, "Imagine the nonsense . . ." Charles and Ritz, *Brother Ray*, 22.

p. 28, "I could just feel . . ." Ben Fong-Torres, "Ray in His Own Words," *Rolling Stone*, http://www.rollingstone.com/news/story/_/id/6128247?rnd=1105564500685&has-player=true&version=6.0.12.1040, January 18, 1973 (accessed July 2004).

p. 30, "My ears were sponges . . ." David Ritz, *Ray Charles Ultimate Hits Collection* (Los Angeles: Rhino Records, 1999), 10.

p. 31, "I just do like a bat . . ." Michael Lydon, *Ray Charles: Man and Music* (Edinburgh: Mojo Books, 2000), 99.

p. 32, "Nothing had hit me . . ." Ibid., 23.

p. 32, "Your mama spent . . ." Charles and Ritz, *Brother Ray*, 61.

p. 33, "That was one of the . . ." Ibid., 67.

CHAPTER THREE: Jammin'

p. 36, "And I could understand . . ." Charles and Ritz, *Brother Ray*, 69.

p. 39, "[R. C.] was a bouncy . . ." Lydon, *Ray Charles: Man and Music*, 42.

p. 40, "You either cut the mustard . . ." Charles and Ritz, *Brother Ray*, 80.

p. 44, "I ate, slept and drank . . ." "Ray Charles Biography," http://www.raycharles.com.

p. 45, "Ain't good enough, kid . . ." Lydon, *Ray Charles: Man and Music*, 43.

p. 45, "At the time . . ." Ritz, *Ray Charles Ultimate Hits Collection*, 14.

p. 46, "Nobody had to . . ." Ibid., 12.

CHAPTER FOUR: Chitlin Circuit

p. 49, "as well as my . . ." Charles and Ritz, *Brother Ray*, 96.

p. 50, "They did everything . . ." Paul de Barros, *Jackson Street*

After Hours: The Roots of Jazz in Seattle (Berkeley, CA: Publishers Group West, 1993), introduction.

p. 51, "Someone asked me . . ." Ritz, *Ray Charles Ultimate Hits Collection*, 13.

p. 53, "Ray Charles was a man . . ." Quincy Jones, *Q: The Autobiography of Quincy Jones* (New York: Doubleday, 2001), 43.

p. 56, "Good God almighty!" Charles and Ritz, *Brother Ray*, 100.

p. 63, "It's detestable when you live it," Whitney Balliett, "Profiles," *New Yorker*, March 28, 1970, 62.

p. 63, *"White side!"* Charles and Ritz, *Brother Ray*, 125.

p. 64, "I said, 'Hey Jack . . .'" National Visionary Leadership Interview, 46.

CHAPTER FIVE: Hallelujah! The Big Time

p. 67, "I thought Ray Charles . . ." Robert Palmer, *The Birth of Soul* (New York: Atlantic, 1991), liner notes.

p. 68, "We'll take care of . . ." National Visionary Leadership Interview, 48.

p. 69, "[S]top this Nat Cole . . ." Fong-Torres, "Ray in His Own Words."

p. 69, "The cats were so . . ." Charles and Ritz, *Brother Ray*, 143.

p. 71, "the blasphemous idea . . ." Anthony Breznican, "Ray Charles Remembered as an Innovator," *Black Pages Today,* http://www.blackpagestoday.com/raycharlesdeadat73.html (accessed January 19, 2005)

p. 72, "There's a towering difference . . ." Palmer, *The Birth of Soul.*

p. 73, "His whole approach . . ." Ibid.

p. 74-75, "I got criticism . . ." Ibid.

p. 78, "Crying's always been a way . . ." Chet Cooper, "Ray Charles Interview," *Ability,* September 19, 2001, http://www.abilitymagazine.com/charles_interview.html

(accessed January 19, 2005)

p. 81, "I said to the band . . ." Charles & Ritz, *Brother Ray*, 191.

CHAPTER SIX: The Hits Keep Coming

p. 85, "He had the total sound . . ." Ritz, *Ray Charles Ultimate Hits Collection*, 19.

p. 87, "I didn't want to leave . . ." Charles & Ritz, *Brother Ray*, 197.

p. 87, "Corny? Hell, yes . . ." Ritz, *Ray Charles Ultimate Hits Collection*, 26.

p. 90, "I was only interested . . ." Charles & Ritz, *Brother Ray*, 223.

p. 91, "Why shucks . . ." Robert Sheldon, *The Country Music Story* (Secaucus, NJ: Castle Books, 1966), 106.

p. 93, "Ray Charles did more . . ." Jim Patterson, "Nashville Sound: Ray Charles Revisits One of His Classics," *The Oak Ridger*, November 6, 1998, http://www.oakridger.com/stories/110698/stt_9.html (Accessed January 19, 2005).

p. 93, "After a week . . ." Lydon, *Ray Charles: Man and Music*, 220.

p. 94, "That would really be . . ." Thompson, *Life,* 60.

p. 95, "I promised myself . . ." Charles & Ritz, *Brother Ray*, 156-157.

p. 96-97, "Beyond restraint now . . ." Lydon, *Ray Charles: Man and Music*, 204.

p. 97, "A sane train of thought . . ." Ibid., 228.

p. 98-99, "When you use . . ." Charles & Ritz, *Brother Ray*, 249.

CHAPTER SEVEN: Under the Rainbow

p. 100, "When you grow up . . ." Lydon, *Ray Charles: Man and Music*, 221.

p. 102, "The North was . . ." Charles & Ritz, *Brother Ray*, 165.

p. 103, "[w]hen folks start . . ." Lydon, *Ray Charles: Man and Music*, 274.

p. 105-106, "This kid really loves me . . ." Ibid., 253.

p. 106, "I vomited and vomited . . ." Charles and Ritz, *Brother Ray,* 257.

p. 106, "There's no luck . . ." Lydon, *Ray Charles: Man and Music,* 255.

p. 107, "Uh-huh . . ." Ibid., 267.

p. 108, "wasn't denying . . ." Charles and Ritz, *Brother Ray,* 236.

p. 109, "nearly sick with . . . she just burned," Ibid., 283.

p. 110, "surest way to get . . ." Charles and Ritz, *Brother Ray*, 228.

p. 113, "Everyone at Motown . . ." Ritz, *Ray Charles Ultimate Hits Collection,* 31.

p. 113, "Just the way black folks sing . . ." Charles and Ritz, *Brother Ray*, 269.

p. 113, "Soul is when . . ." Thompson, *Life,* 58.

p. 114, "Sometimes I've clipped . . ." Ritz, *Ray Charles Ultimate Hits Collection,* 6.

p. 114, "My mother said . . ." Lydon, *Ray Charles: Man and Music*, 207.

CHAPTER EIGHT: He's the Right One, Baby!

p. 122, "I'm the first to say . . ." Ritz, *Ray Charles Ultimate Hits Collection,* 34.

p. 122, "That's like the Statue . . ." David Breskin, "There Comes a Time When We Heed a Certain Call," *Life*, April, 1985.

p. 123, "I've put my hand on . . ." Ibid.

p. 127, "could hear a rat pee on cotton," Bill Carpenter, "Mabel John and Candi Statton Remember the Late Ray Charles,"

Soul-Patrol, September 15, 2004, http://www.soul-patrol.com/soul/bro_ray.htm (accessed January 19, 2005).

p. 127, "Most people take . . ." Cooper, "Ray Charles Interview."

p. 128, "I'm too old . . ." Lydon, *Ray Charles: Man and Music,* 346.

p. 128, "It's amazing to watch . . ." "A Masters Voice: Conversations with Ray Charles," *Yamaha All Access*, Winter 2004, http://www.yamaha.com/publications/allaccess/winter2004/raycharles.html (accessed January 13, 2005).

p. 129, "I don't understand . . ." Charles and Ritz, *Brother Ray*, 307.

CHAPTER NINE: Final Verse

p. 130-131, "Been saying this . . ." Ritz, *Ray Charles Ultimate Hits Collection,* 4.

p. 132, "You know, I think . . ." Cooper, "Ray Charles Interview."

p. 133, "He'd know it if . . ." Guy Martin, "Blue Genius," *Esquire*, May 1986.

p. 134, "You know you're getting . . ." Cooper, "Ray Charles Interview."

p. 135, "Your band is all . . ." Staff news article, "Stars Sing the Praises of Late Soul Genius Ray Charles," Agence France Presse, September 30, 2004. http://www.ent-today.com/music/oct04/mu100804_rc.htm (accessed January 13, 2005).

p. 136, "There are ups and downs . . ." David Hoffman, "Interview with Ray Charles Trumpet Soloist David Hoffman," interviewed by Paul Adams, Paul Adams Music, http://www.pauladams.org/davidhoffmaninterview.htm (accessed January 13, 2005).

p. 136, "On those best nights, . . ." David Hoffman, "A Personal Remembrance of Ray Charles." David Hoffman Jazz.

http://www.davidhoffmanjazz.com/rayobit.htm (accessed September 2004).

p. 137, "I thought I had . . ." Charles and Ritz, *Brother Ray*, 225.

p. 137, "Circuit Breakers?" Lydon, *Ray Charles: Man and Music*, 396.

p. 137-138, "I've known times . . ." Andrew Gumbel, "The Pioneering Musician Who Eased the Pain of Depression at the Piano," *Independent Digital Newspaper*, http://enjoyment. independent.co.uk/music/news/story.jsp?story=530315, June 11, 2004. (accessed January 13, 2005).

p. 138, "This is a girl's bike . . ." Ray Charles, "What I've Learned: Ray Charles," interviewed by Mike Sager, *Esquire*, http://www.esquire.com/features/learned/030801_mwi_charles. html, August 2003 (accessed January 19, 2005).

p. 139, "a soul brother . . ." *Genius Loves Company*, (Beverly Hills, CA: Concord Records, 2004), liner notes.

p. 140, "Rockets went off . . ." "Musicians Honor Charles on Tribute Album," Associated Press/ABC 7 News, August 30, 2004 http://www.wjla.com/news/stories/0804/169632.html (accessed January 19, 2005).

Bibliography

Balliett, Whitney. "Profiles." *New Yorker,* March 28, 1970.

Breznican, Anthony. "Ray Charles Remembered as an Innovator." *Black Pages Today* (Associated Press), June 12, 2004. http://www.blackpagestoday.com/raycharlesdeadat73.html.

Carpenter, Bill. "Mabel John and Candi Statton Remember the Late Ray Charles." *Soul-Patrol*, September 15, 2004. http://www.soul-patrol.com/soul/bro_ray.htm .

Charles, Ray. "Ray Charles Biography." RayCharles.com: The Official Site, http://www.raycharles.com.

———. "Ray Charles Interview." By Chet Cooper. *Ability,* September 19, 2001, http://www.abilitymagazine.com/charles_interview.html (Accessed January 19, 2005).

———. "Ray Charles Interview." National Visionary Leadership Project, http://www.visionaryproject.com/NVLPmemberTier/visionariesT1/VisionaryPages/CharlesRay/transcript.pdfinterview, 2002.

———. "What I've Learned: Ray Charles." By Mike Sager. *Esquire,* August 2003. http://www.esquire.com/features/learned/030801_mwi_charles.html.

——— and David Ritz. *Brother Ray*. New York: Da Capo Press, 1992.

de Barros, Paul. *Jackson Street After Hours: The Roots of Jazz in Seattle.* Berkeley, CA: Publishers Group West, 1993.

Fong-Torres, Ben. "Ray in His Own Words." *Rolling Stone*, January 18, 1973. http://www.rollingstone.com/news/story/_/id/6128247?rnd=1105564500685&has-player=true&version=6.0.12.1040.

Genius Loves Company (Liner Notes). Beverly Hills, CA: Concord Records, 2004.

Gumbel, Andrew. "The Pioneering Musician Who Eased the Pain of Depression at the Piano." *Independent Digital Newspaper*, June 11, 2004. http://enjoyment.independent.co.uk/music/news/story.jsp?story=530315.

Hoffman, David. "Interview with Ray Charles Trumpet Soloist David Hoffman." By Paul Adams, Paul Adams Music, http://www.pauladams.org/davidhoffmaninterview.htm.

————. "A Personal Remembrance of Ray Charles." David Hoffman Jazz. http://www.davidhoffmanjazz.com/rayobit.htm.

Jones, Quincy. *Q: The Autobiography of Quincy Jones.* New York: Doubleday, 2001.

Lydon, Michael. *Ray Charles: Man and Music.* Edinburgh: Mojo Books, 2000.

Martin, Guy. "Blue Genius." *Esquire*, May 1986.

"A Masters Voice: Conversations with Ray Charles." *Yamaha All Access*, Winter 2004. http://www.yamaha.com/publications/allaccess/winter2004/raycharles.html.

"Musicians Honor Charles on Tribute Album." Associated Press/ABC 7 News, August 30, 2004. http://www.wjla.com/news/stories/0804/169632.html.

Palmer, Robert. *The Birth of Soul* (Liner Notes). New York: Atlantic, 1991.

Patterson, Jim. "Nashville Sound: Ray Charles Revisits One of His Classics." *The Oak Ridger*, November 6, 1998, http://

www.oakridger.com/stories/110698/stt_9.html.

Ritz, David. *Ray Charles Ultimate Hits Collection* (Liner Notes). Los Angeles: Rhino Records, 1999.

Sheldon, Robert. *The Country Music Story*. Secaucus, NJ: Castle Books, 1966.

"Stars Sing the Praises of Late Soul Genius Ray Charles." Agence France Presse. http://www.ent-today.com/music/oct04/mu100804_rc.htm, September 30, 2004

Thompson, Thomas. "Music Soaring in a Darkened World." *Life*, July 19, 1996.